Ranger

Ranger
The Adventurous Life of Robert Rogers of the Rangers

Allan Nevins

LEONAUR

Ranger: the Adventurous Life of Robert Rogers of the Rangers
by Allan Nevins

Leonaur is an imprint of Oakpast Ltd

Material original to this edition and presentation of the
text in this form copyright © 2011 Oakpast Ltd

ISBN: 978-0-85706-703-6 (hardcover)
ISBN: 978-0-85706-704-3 (softcover)

http://www.leonaur.com

Publisher's Notes

Contents

CHAPTER 1

Birth and Early Life

We have no historical background of family or lineage against which to place Robert Rogers, and about his cradle hangs a cloud which research has not found it easy to dispel. He first saw the light of day on November 17th 1731, in the frontier cabin of James Rogers, a sturdy farmer of Methuen in upper Massachusetts. Of his mother we know only that her name was Mary. His birth is the first fact in the family annals which the local records have preserved, and whence his parents and three older brothers had come, or what had been their previous history, remains a secret.[1] As to even the stock from which he sprung, whether English, Scotch, or Scotch-Irish[2] we have only the tradition that it was his father who, in later

Years, named a piece of land upon which they settled Mountalona, after a loved spot among the Presbyterian hills of County Dery.[3] The absence of any note of James Rogers'

1. *Methuen Town Records; New Hampshire Province Deeds,* XXXIIII, 20. Rogers three elder brothers were Daniel, who lived some years in Dunbarton, New Hampshire, as a farmer; Samuel and James, who became an ensign and later a captain in the rangers commanded by Robert Rogers, married Margaret McGregor, daughter of the Rev. David McGregor of Londonderry, New Hampshire, and fleeing to Canada on the outbreak of the Revolution, founded the influential and wealthy Canadian branch of the family.
2. There are many families of Rogers' identified with the early history of Essex County, Massachusetts, where the name is of course generally one of the most common in New England, whether among the Puritans—two who came in the Mayflower were named Rogers—or among the Scotch-Irish who began to enter the northern colonies in 1719. It will be remembered that one of the seventeenth century presidents of Harvard College was John Rogers. A James Rogers of Londonderry who settled at Dunbarton (Starkstown or Gorhamstown) about twelve years after Robert's father moved there was long confused with the latter. (continued on next page)

presence in Methuen before 1737 makes it certain that he was but a newcomer in the town, having arrived probably a year or two earlier along one of the forest-girdled bridle-paths which stretched from the coast settlements westward, along the Merrimac River. In a double sense, therefore, Robert Rogers was born into a pioneer environment; for Methuen lay as an outpost for all the northern and western section of the province, verging upon a wilderness that extended deep and unbroken to the French villages along the St. Francis, and he had entered a household before which still lay in large part the task of wresting a living from the woods and untamed fields.

The community of Methuen was a happy one for a growing and struggling family.[4] Virtually a western extension of Haverhill, from which it had enjoyed but five years separation, it constituted, with the older township, a connected belt of settlement along the upper bank of the Merrimac, roughly fifteen miles long and four miles wide; a still wild region facing the brawling little river, and only sparsely dotted with log huts and their surrounding clearings. Upon the present site of the city of Haverhill huddled the homes of a compact village, and elsewhere at central points rose rough meetinghouses. While the family had neighbours in plenty, especially along the rutted and stony cart-tracks which traversed hill and thicket towards Haverhill, their homes were scattered over miles of ground in the roomy manner characteristic of Anglo-Saxon settlement, and left ample space for a free agricultural and sylvan life.

The Naumkeag, the Accomenta, and the Agawam Indians lay toward the French possessions in a cloud threatening enough to such an exposed community; but since Queen

There were so many English families of Rogers' in Essex that there is room for serious doubt whether Rogers was not of that people. See Josiah H. Drummond, *The John Rogers Families in Plymouth and Vicinity*. Read before the Maine Historical Society, Portland, Maine, 1895, n.p. *James Rogers of Londonderry and James Rogers of Dunbarton*, Manchester, N. H., 1897.
3. John Farmer and J. B. Moore, *A Gazetteer of the State of New Hampshire*, Concord, 1823-31; p. 121. Also Caleb Mark, *History of Dunbarton, New Hampshire*, Concord, 1860. Also *New Hampshire State Papers*, XXVII, 197, where it is called Montetony.
4. J. S. Howe, *Historical Sketch of Methuen,* Methuen, 1901, p. 9-17. George Wingate Chase, *History of Haverhill*, Haverhill, 1861, chapters VI-X.

Anne's war they had committed none but the most trivial depredations.[5] Game abounded, and the nearby Spicket and Merrimac swarmed with salmon and shad.[6]

The beauty of the forested and hilly country, broken by jutted capes of bare smooth upland and by river meadows whose moist black earth afforded a luxuriant sickle-grass for the cattle and deer, was evident to anyone who had eyes for it.[7] Nor, externally rough and picturesquely wild as it often seemed, was the land really unproductive. By labour certainly hard, but as certainly fruitful, it could be brought to exchange its elm and hemlock for apple and pear, its wild blackberry for patches of pumpkin and turnips, and its timber and bush for Indian corn and timothy.

To such institutions, moreover, as ministered to its higher social needs, the township paid the same zealous attention that was characteristic of the whole Puritan colony. The general Court's ordinance of division[8] from Haverhill had provided that within three years from 1725 the citizens should erect a house for public worship, and settle in it "a learned orthodox minister of good conversation;" and after a brief period of contentious wrangling over the location of the church and the choice of a pastor, a minister was inducted into office at a salary little short of munificent for so poor a community.

Of equal importance to the householders was the maintenance of the public schools, for which fifty acres of land. Had been set aside at the creation of the village. In the year of Robert's birth, the citizens voted to appoint three schoolmasters, each of whom should conduct classes in his own home for one month in midwinter. In 1735 it was resolved to erect a suitable structure to house the growing number of children, and a log school was

---

5. J. G. Whittier, *Prose Works*, Boston, 188, II, 368.
6. J. S. Howe, *Sketch of Methuen*, p. 4. For generations after apprentices commonly stipulated in their articles of indenture that they should not have to eat salmon more than six times weekly.
7. J. G. Whittier, *Prose Works*, I and II, *Legends and Sketches*. Whittier was of Haverhill. H. D. Thoreau, *A Week on the Concord and Merrimac Rivers*.
8. This ordinance of division was passed in December, 1725. See Howe, *Sketch of Methuen*, p. 10.

soon after placed, for convenience of access, and surety of pastoral supervision, beside the church.[9] Robert's three older brothers were able to avail themselves of this education from its very beginnings, and he himself soon after; for no townsman could retain even his younger children at home without incurring the decided disapproval of his neighbours. Reading was taught from the Bible, with perhaps a well-thumbed copy of the New England primer, and writing and accounts upon carefully smoothed and stripped sections of birch bark. Under the rigid application enforced by a sternly dignified master, and amid community, acquisition of a serviceable modicum of knowledge was rapid.

Thus under circumstances of which it is not hard to form some conception, Robert passed at Methuen the first eight years of his life. His home was the typical frontier cabin of the period, built of roughly-squared logs, with a loft above and two comfortable rooms below. In the great living room, puncheon floored, stood the inevitable spinning-wheel, the clothes-chest, the rough table and stiff chairs; at one side rose the large, unvarnished dresser, the pewter and china sparkling in serried rows upon it; a shelf above supported its Bible and a few cherished books, chiefly devotional, and perhaps mingled with a handful of polemical tracts; and at one end was built the spacious fireplace, whose heavy andirons admitted eight-foot logs to crackle on the hearth, filling the apartment on the bitterest winter night with radiance and warmth. The firelight or sunlight playing into the other room lit up the drawers and shelves fastened to the timbers, caught the glint of woollen coverlets on the beds, and sparkled bravely back from the polished queen's arm that hung, its battles with the French long over, from pegs driven deep into the wall. Above all, festooning the ceiling in both rooms, were strings of dried fruit, bunches of herbs, links of corn tied by the husks, and even sausages and bacon. The heavy diamond-paned windows were crossed inside with wooden bars, and a portable ladder reached the loft. As a boy

---

9. Howe, *Sketch of Methuen*. Chase, *History of Haverhill*, p. 173. G. C. Bush, *History of Education in New Hampshire*, Washington, 1898, p. 55. James O. Lyford, *History of Canterbury, New Hampshire*, Concord, 1912, Chapter XIX.

Robert knew the hard fare of such a home—game, Indian meal sweetened with berries into samp, and simple vegetables; and as he grew older he was impressed into the less arduous of the daily tasks about the busy household, or played with his brothers in the neighbouring forests.[10] He became familiar with the gliding naked forms of the savages, passing to town to barter or steal; with the fur-clad hunter, bent under a load of steaming venison; with the rough lumberman, the fisher, the mower along the wide meadow marshes, and perhaps even the jolly mariners who came up by ship to Haverhill. He heard stories of the northern tribes, varying from vivid recitals of the attacks of thirty years before to peaceful legends of the half-mystical grandeur of their old chief Passonconway; echoes of the hostile presence of the French to the north; and descriptions of the wildcat, the bear, the wolf, and the grisly catamount. He was thus awakening fully to the frontier life about him when, in 1739, his parents resolved upon a new step

James and Mary Rogers had arrived at Methuen too late to share in the general distribution of the town's land, and hence had obtained there no extensive holdings.[11] To the north and west, beyond the bend of the Merrimac and in its upper valley, lay a broad tract of rich territory just becoming available through the liberal grants of the General Court. Here they naturally began to look for such a breadth of acres as would ensure them a more generous competence, in especial, probably, the birth of a fourth son in 1734 and of a daughter in 1736.[12] In these years they heard more and more of the delectable lands, for they were rapidly being explored and surveyed, and a thin line of settlers was streaming up the east bank of the river and breaking across it at a score of places into what is now New Hampshire. Rumford, lying fifty miles up on the left side, was incorporated in 1734

---

10. J. G. Whittier, *Prose Works,* II, 396 and elsewhere.

11. Howe, *Sketch of Methuen,* p. 7.

12. Drummond, *James Rogers of Londonderry and James Rogers of Dunbarton* p. 11. The brother was named Richard; he afterward became a captain in Robert Rogers' Rangers, and died in the service, at Fort William Henry, in 1767, of smallpox. The sister was named Mary. Another brother, John, and another sister, Catherine, were born after the family's removal to the north.

with nearly one hundred families, and in the same month the township immediately below it was granted to veterans of the Narragansett war. Londonderry and Chester, intervening between Rumford and Methuen, were already filled with Scotch-Irish, and Suncook, lying athwart the river near them, had been parcelled-out to settlers ten years previously.[13] Amid an exploitation of new territory that thus yearly became more general, Rogers was upon the alert to buy advantageously.

His choice was a bold one. On November 24th, 1738, for the sum of £110, he bought off Zaccheus Lovewell of Canterbury a tract called Lovell's Farm, comprising nearly four hundred acres sixteen miles south and west of Rumford, at a greater distance beyond the Merrimac than any settler had yet gone.[14] The farm was a portion of a larger area which Lovewell and five associates had secured in 1735, but which lay so well outside the direct currents of immigration, which in Massachusetts were hugging the colonial boundary, and in New Hampshire the Merrimac River, that even its proprietors knew little of its character. By 1737 two cottagers only had crept timidly westward a few miles from Rumford, and although in the same year the whole township in which Lovewell's grant lay was assigned to one Shubal Goreham and his associates, no colonists had yet proposed to settle upon it.[15] Rogers, however, who had never known the border except in time of peace, was irresistibly attracted by one salient feature of the new site: high hills and unbroken forests lay about, but down between them crept and expanded a broad meadow, partly natural interval land and partly cleared by beavers, over which billowed a field of rich grass. He prevailed upon one of his neighbours, Joseph Pudney, a former shopkeeper of Salem, and more recently, with his six stalwart sons, the cultiva-

13. *New Hampshire State Papers*, XXIV, 59, 108, 233.
14. *New Hampshire Province Deeds*, XXXVIII, 20. The land was granted to Lovewell in recognition of his services under his brother, Captain John Lovewell, in the campaign against the Main Indians which culminated in the latter's victorious death at Pigwacket. In 1737 Captain William Tyng, the first soldier to use snowshoes in campaigning against the Indians, was given land a few miles southeast of Lovewell's settlement, which he, like Gorham, failed to colonize.
15. *New Hampshire State Papers*, XXIV, 80 (with plan).

tor of several farms near Haverhill, to accompany him. Pudney, an unlettered man, was already growing old, but he possessed a practical turn of mind, and his assistance, and that of his family would be almost indispensable in opening a new country.[16]

Early in the spring of 1739, when Robert was eight years old, the two families removed to their new home; driving their cattle before them, and conveying as best they could, in the absence of roads, their movable goods.[17]

The tract upon which they found themselves offered several wholly novel advantages in agriculture.[18] From the broad top of the highest hill, near the point where Rogers actually laid his hearthstone, the crests of the White Mountains, nearly a hundred miles to the north, could be seen on clear days "like great bright clouds above the horizon." There were many small lakes in the township, emptying to the east by trout-brooks which fed down under thick coverts of alder and birch to the bickering Merrimac, seven miles away; and the rougher land was heavily forested. The chief advantage of the district, however, consisted in its smooth upland meadows, a relief especially welcome to tenants used to the broken ground and marshy arable land of Methuen. Upon the largest and most elevated of these Rogers and Pudney commenced the construction of their houses, and during the summer months erected two buildings of hewn logs at no great distance from one another. Their families once safely installed, they were able, before the beginning of winter, to provide two hasty shelters for their stock. Their houses were in a forlornly chilly solitude, broken only by the presence within the neighbouring valleys of some small camps of friendly Indians.

In this changed seat the families prospered for the next few years. Pudney had bought no land, but had shared the purchase of Rogers; and he or his neighbour secured an additional plot

---

16. *Essex County Record*, Salem, Massachusetts. *New Hampshire State Papers*, XXVII, 190: "Joseph Pudney, his mark."

17. *New Hampshire State Papers*, XXVII, 190.

18. Descriptions will be found in Jeremy Belknap, *History of New Hampshire*, Boston, 1791-2; Farmer and Moore, *New Hampshire Gazetteer*; Caleb Stark, *History of Dunbarton*; D. H. Hurd, *History of Merrimac and Belknap Counties, New Hampshire*, Philadelphia, 1885.

nearby upon a promissory note and they jointly began clearing it for tillage. Some neighbouring fields were being already fenced, and during the summer herdsmen drove fattening cattle upon them from farms lower along the Merrimac, retiring again to the south, however, at the approach of winter. Two orchards were set out by the pioneers, and by 1745 had so prospered as to bear fruit; one hundred acres of meadow were fenced, and mown or grazed annually; and as many more were devoted to grain.[19] In the larger tasks the two households gave one another the assistance that made extensive farming operations possible. Each year the bays of the barn were crammed with hay for winter fodder; each year the older sons bent beneath the midsummer sun to the cutting of the wheat or rye; each year the care of the orchard and the cutting of brush, with hunting and trapping, filled in the portions of the twelve-month not devoted to seeding and harvesting. Even after the first storms of winter there was no relaxation of labour. Long after,[20] Robert told in London of how as a boy he gathered the shoots of alder and birch, and bearing them home in fagots, bound them into brooms, and carried them over ice and snow fifteen miles through the woods to the nearest marketplace—the town of Rumford. Hither from Lovell's Farm led only a blazed path, winding beneath the sombre shade over hill and valley, through copse and brake, skirting the ridges and fording streams, until it came in view of the brief, uneven streets of rough houses, and the edge of the Merrimac river beyond. Upon the town's mills and stores the isolated pioneers depended for their scanty store of purchased provisions, and possibly upon its schools and churches for meagre mental and spiritual guidance. They kept intact also the links between themselves and Methuen, for during several autumns, one marked by so great a drought that farmers elsewhere imported hay from England, the elder Rogers bought or took at a rental cattle in Haverhill and drove them north to be wintered.[21] But in general the families

19. *New Hampshire State Papers*, XXVII, 192.
20. John Farmer and J. B. Moore, *Historical and Miscellaneous Collections*, Concord, 1823-31, I, 240.
21. Hurd, *History of Merrimac and Belknap Counties*, p. 292.

were self-sufficing social and economic units, and as such felt but little hardship in their position.

The outbreak of King George's War in 1744 brought the first sharp reversal of their fortunes, blighting their hopes for a serene continuance of years of apple-growing and hay cropping, threatening the little property they had amassed, and finally making them tremble for their very lives. The descent of the war, however, with its inevitable concomitants of Indian massacre and Canadian pillage, was not unexpected, and such isolated settlers as Rogers and Pudney had ample time in which to prepare or remove to the towns. Even if the French attack on the border, mercifully delayed more than a year after the beginning of the conflict, had come early, no distant holm or hamlet would have been taken unaware; for when in June, cresting a general wave of alarm, the couriers rode forth from Boston with the news that had just come by ship, warning all New England to gird herself, the settlements had already begun their preparations—nowhere with more vigour than at Rumford. Even while governor Benning Wentworth[22] was declaring to a special session of the Assembly at Portsmouth that "the naked condition of our inland frontiers requires your compassionate regard," sixty-seven families at the centre to which Rogers and Pudney looked for protection had sent to the capital a memorial praying that, inasmuch as the buildings of the town "were compact, properly-formed for defence, and well-situated for a barrier, lying on the Merrimac only fifteen miles below the confluence of the two main river gangways of the Canadians to the frontiers of the provinces," the settlement be created the seat of a general garrison.[23] Though the petition remained unanswered, a number of the strongest houses in the town were fortified as places of instant refuge, the fields were worked by men in armed companies, and during the summer a scouting squad was kept ranging the woods to the north. Not, however, until the autumn of the next year, 1745, the French begin the inspiration of their

22. *New Hampshire Province Papers* V, 709.
23. James O. Lyford (editor), *History of Concord, New Hampshire,* Concord, 1903, I, 166.

savage allies to border ravages; when, incensed and humiliated by Pepperell's capture of Louisbourg, they commenced a horrifying series of outrages along the upper Connecticut, and in northern New York. During the first two summers of the war Rogers and Pudney remained upon the fields that constituted their all, their only danger being from bands of the weak neighbouring tribes, now withdrawing resentfully from the vicinity of the settlements, against whom their own numbers constituted a sufficient protection; but in early October of the second year a heavy attack was made upon Westmoreland, directly west of Rumford on the Connecticut, in November Saratoga was sacked and burnt, and simultaneously Crown Point became the basis of operation for a score of strong Indian parties. Outlying farms were everywhere deserted, and the inhabitants rallied to the nearest villages for defence.

At the beginning of winter in 1745 Rogers and Pudney seem to have come in to the shelter of Rumford. Here they remained for three years, able to devote only the most intermittent attention to their farms, so unceasing were the inroads of the savages; but in an environment which gave the boy Robert his first invaluable lessons in the art of woodland warfare. The persistency with which the savages pushed the struggle to their very doors is well set forth in local and other documents. In the months of May and June, according to a French paper, yet preserved, thirty five different war-parties of Abenaki and Ottawa were sent out from Crown Point to ravage the frontier;[24] and on May 5th zealous Captain Goffe wrote from Rumford, "about two o clock in the morning. . . . the Indians are all about. There was never more need of soldiers than now. It is enough to make one's blood boil to see our fellow creatures killed and taken up on every quarter."[25] On May 15th, 1746, by order of the general assembly, three citizens of Rumford distributed its families and those that had taken refuge in the town among ten garrison houses, assigning to one James and Samuel Rogers, and to another Joseph Pudney and his sons William, Henry, and Samuel.[26] Up and down the Merrimac men worked in the fields, during this and the following summer, only in large companies, with arms always by their sides. Even at church the settlers carried their guns into the pews, and the minister prayed with his piece resting against the pulpit. Bands of rangers patrolled the woods of the neighbourhood. To the poor the towns distributed free powder, bullets, flints, and muskets. No shot might be fired after sunset.[27] On 20th May, 1747, there was so incisive an attack upon the town of Suncook, immediately below Rumford and to the east of Lovell's farm, that the province ordered out a trebly-augmented body of scouts to safeguard the upper reaches of the river.[28] Those even of comparatively sheltered regions who were forced to take risks in preserving the fruit of their acres often suffered for their temerity; and the people of Pembroke, east of the Merrimac, complained that they "lived so much exposed to the Indian enemy that they got their bread at the peril of their lives, by reason of the sword of the wilderness." In July of 1747, when the aged Joseph Pudney had his arm broken by a shot while carrying "a wooden bottle beer" from a village garrison to men at work in the fields, the alarm became extraordinary, and only a reinforcement of thirty men sent by Wentworth to Rumford permitted a continuance of hay-mowing, then just begun, in the vicinity of town.[29]

Nor until the end of the year did the frequency of Indian aggressions at all abate.

During these two adventurous years the boy Robert Rogers, for his age remarkably tall and sturdy, not merely bore the excited interest of youth in all that was passing about him, but found means also to mingle actively in the heady current

24. Parkman, *A Half-Century of Conflict*, II, 214. All references to Francis Parkman's Works are to the Frontenac Edition, Boston, 1905; except to the *Conspiracy of Pontiac*, where the pages refer to the Boston edition of 1851.

25. *New Hampshire Province Papers*, V, 800.

26. Lyford, *History of Concord*, I, 170-173. Nathaniel Bouton, *History of Concord*, Concord, 1856, p. 154. The two Rogers' were assigned to the house of Timothy Walker, Jr., at what is now Main and Thorndike streets, Concord.

27. Potter, *Military History of New Hampshire, New Hampshire Adjutant General's Report*, Concord, 1866, I, 38; Bouton's *History of Concord*, p. 150.

28. Potter, *Military History of New Hampshire*, I, 99.

29. Lyford, *History of Concord*, I, 180. *New Hampshire Province Papers*, V, 880.

of the war's events. In winter, when even the boldest hunters stirred little abroad, he may have been in school; in summer he participated in both the village harvest and the village military expeditions. In August, 1746, when at fifteen he was not yet liable for militia duty, he was impressed into the ranks by a sudden exigency, an attack made on the tenth of that month upon a detachment of a local scouting company, as it was being transferred along a forest lane from Rumford to a fortified house two miles west, resulting in the killing and scalping[30] of seven men, in the very heart of garrisons and patrols, and at not a mile's distance from a whole company of soldiery. Amid the general consternation Robert and his brother Samuel, with two of the Pudneys, enlisted and served until the end of September, ranging over all the country below Lake Winnipesaukee, but seeing little real fighting.[31] Similarly in August of the second year Robert enlisted again in a company of rangers, and campaigned for six weeks under Captain Ebenezer Eastman. The body of which he made one scoured the woods north and west of his home for thirty miles, operating over territory with which he had become thoroughly familiar, and engaging, upon one or two occasions, in a light skirmish.[32] At various times the hardy lad may have done sentinel duty about the town. During the winter of 1747-8 the intensity of the war lessened so perceptibly that Rogers and his old neighbour felt that they might securely return to Lovell's Farm. and at a very early date in the spring they were once more settled in their old homes, ready to recommence farming operations. For some months fewer and fewer rumours of the proximity of the Indians had disturbed the settlements; since the capture of Fort Massachusetts two years before no military event of any moment had occurred in America; and European affairs were steadily pointing toward peace. Unfortunately, one of the last strokes of the

30. Lyford, *History of Concord*, I, 175.
31. Potter, *Military History of New Hampshire,* I, 95. During the summer of 1747 thirty soldiers were on guard at Rumford; in the autumn a large party of Indians hung about the southwest part of town, killing cattle, until driven off. Jacob Moore, *Annals of Concord*, Concord, 1824.
32. Potter, *Military History of New Hampshire,* I, 99.

war was destined to touch the fortunes of the pioneers most severely. Toward evening of one day in April a band of savages was discovered to be lurking in the vicinity of Rumford. The alarm was given, and while messengers notified other outlying cottagers, two friends of Rogers and Pudney traced their way along the blazed path through the forest blackness to warn them of the impending danger. Upon receipt of the alarming intelligence, the two families precipitately abandoned their homes, and beat a speedy retreat to the nearest garrison. The next day, accompanied by an adequate guard from the town, they returned to drive their cattle in to safety. They were too late. The Indians had plundered and burnt their houses, destroyed their barns, killed a heifer and a steer belonging to Rogers, and spread such devastation through their orchard that but a single tree remained standing; and when the settlers turned from the smoking ashes and wasted acres in pursuit, the forest had swallowed the marauders up.

Although this disastrous and unexpected attack virtually ended the partisan fighting in that region, the disheartened Rogers and Pudney spent the remainder of the year in Suncook and Rumford, and from that distance planted and reaped what they might.[33] In October, 1748, the peace of Aix-la-Chapelle was finally signed, and husbandry, industry, and colonization could once more move forward unchecked in the valley of the Merrimac.

Social conditions along the upper valley changed rapidly after 1748; and it was into a country filling with settlers, and brightened by new hopes of prosperity, that James Rogers moved back upon Lovell's Farm a year later, setting Robert and his elder brothers once more at their wonted tasks. Indeed, the inpouring of fresh colonists into the region threatened for a time his tenure of the land for which he had toiled so hard. He had purchased it from the Massachusetts General Court; and now came Scotch farmers from east of the Merrimac, under the leadership of Archibald Stark, bearing more recent and more valid titles

33. Caleb Stark, *History of Dunbarton,* p. 11-13. *New Hampshire State Papers,* XXVII, 190.

from John Mason's heirs. Rogers and Pudney hastened to engage a lawyer at Portsmouth, and in a petition to the proprietors, which several others who had improved land in the neighbourhood reinforced, protested vigorously against any redistribution of acres which should ignore their claims.[34] Their voices were heard, and in the new township of Starkstown, as chartered in December, 1748, to them and to their sons were given adjacent shares on the site of their former fields, and in that part of the tract near which the present town of Dunbarton stands. The terms of the charter provided for the rapid settlement near them of forty-five other families, each with its own house and a clearing of three acres, and reserved also an ample endowment in land for a church and school. Their new neighbours began at once to fell the heavy woods which had lain untroubled about the great meadow, to raise their own house timbers, and to fill the deep woodland paths with the heavy burr of their Scotch accent. By 1751 the community was sparsely but widely peopled, roads were projected to the east and south, and a stimulus had been given to agriculture and land-investment under which Rogers felt a new prosperity. His position became for a time an enviably thriving one, in which he was apparently able to make considerable additions to his estate; for at various dates in 1751 and 1752 he bought most of the holdings of Pudney, and the shares also of several of the Scotch assignees who were prevented from complying with the conditions of the charter.[35]

In this life of a frontier farmer's son Robert Rogers was engaged until the tragic death of his father. In the winter of 1752-3 there came into the country one of James Rogers' old friends, Ebenezer Ayer of Haverhill, celebrated as a successful hunter. He made a camp on Walnut Slope, between Rogers farm and the Merrimac River, and thence pursued his regular avocation of following bears, deer, and other game. In early spring he had once completed a day's sport, and at dusk had repaired to his rude hut; and as it was not yet late, and he had been unsuccessful, he was still on the outlook for a possible wild animal. The

---

34. *New Hampshire State Papers,* XXVII, 190-200.
35. *New Hampshire Province Deeds.*

unfortunate Rogers, dressed from head to foot in bearskins, and already bent by his years of labour, drew near the camp to pay his friend a visit. Deceived by the dusk of evening, the eager hunter shot and so heavily wounded him that, almost before his children or his wife could be brought to his side, he died.[36] Ayer could never after speak of the occurrence without tears. Four of Rogers' sons, however, including Robert, were arrived at manhood's estate, and the future of his family was assured.

In fact, when in 1753 his father's estate was divided, Robert Rogers was twenty-two years old, of extraordinary physique and courage, and completely self-reliant.[37] Since the close of the war he had become an experienced hunter and guide in all the region thereabout, and more recently still had begun to make some agricultural ventures of his own. He had already bought a parcel of wooded land at Merrimac, halfway between Rumford and Methuen, for £70, and upon this, in the summer after his father's death, he began a clearing. A year later (1753) he commenced the cultivation of several acres there, and erected a house and barn, in which, during the autumn, he placed a tenant. He is variously referred to during these two summers as a 'husbandman and yeoman of Rumford' or as a 'housewright of Merrimac,'[38] while we glean from other references to him that his winters, and his spare weeks generally, were spent in hardy and adventurous expeditions northward, as hunter and trader. It is evident that in this latter occupation lay his chief interest. He wrote in a letter, in the only reference he ever made to his youth:

Between the years 1743 and 1753, I was led to a general acquaintance both with the British and French set-

36. Caleb Stark, *History of Dunbarton*, p. 386. J. B. Walker, *Robert Rogers the Ranger,* Boston, 1885, p. 2.

37. "Robert Rogers was six feet in stature, well proportioned, and one of the most athletic youths of his time—well known in all the trials of strength or activity among the young men for several miles around. He was endowed with great presence of mind, intrepidity, perseverance, and possessed a plausible address." Caleb Stark: *Memoir of John Stark* (in Robert Rogers' *Reminiscences of the* French *War,* a garbled edition of the *Journals*), Concord, 1831, p. 387.

38. *New Hampshire Province Deeds,* Parker to Rogers, and others.

tlements in North America, and especially with the un-cultivated desert, the mountains, valleys, rivers, lakes, and several passes that lay between and contiguous to the said settlements. Nor did. I content myself with the accounts I received from the Indians, but travelled over large tracts of country myself, which tended, not more to gratify my curiosity than to inure me to hardship, and to quality me for my later services.[39]

His knowledge of the French towns could easily have been obtained as a petty trader, or a hunter-explorer. The nearest of them lay far to the north and west, above Memphremagog, Champlain, and the headwaters of the St. Francis—a journey to be measured only in days of hard travel. Intercourse between the French and the English, however, was not rare after the close of King George's War; and in one capacity or the other many opportunities must have offered the young man, already locally famed for his strength of limb and knowledge of the wood, to accompany expeditions beyond the border. His love for adventure and his geographical curiosity alone might account for the fact that, like Whittier's grandfather, he had repeatedly watched the moonlight play upon Norman cap and bodiced waist, reeling in dance among the northern pines, or in dusky wigwam or open camp had sat down to the moose and roast corn of a savage board.[40] He may have helped build roads, such as that which Governor Wentworth projected in 1753 to Cohase Meadows, high up on the Connecticut, or have joined the official survey-ing and exploring parties which at this time were penetrating all upper Vermont and New Hampshire. Parkman has suggested that he was probably engaged in smuggling;[41] but in New Eng-land nefarious commerce was then almost exclusively a coast-wise practice, and no such improbable hypothesis is required to explain why a young man of mettle should not always have contented himself with a farmer's sphere.

---

39. Preface to Robert Rogers *Journals*, London, 1765. Similar statements to be found in some of his later memorials,
40. J. G. Whittier, *Snowbound.*
41. Parkman, *Montcalm and Wolfe*, II, 119.

What is to be observed is that when in 1754 he had attained to some maturity, he appreciated fully the resources and temper of English border civilization; he was acquainted with the language and customs of both French and Indians; the forest was a book whose pages he had cultivated until there were few of its problems, its hardships, or its dangers he could not master; and he knew with some intimacy all the land enclosed between the White Mountains, the nearer shore of the St. Lawrence, and the sources of the Hudson. His whole character—his strength, endurance, and initiative, with many rougher and less, admirable traits—was that of a frontiersman. With 1754 there dawned a new epoch in his life.

CHAPTER 2

The French and Indian War

As early as 1753, the summer in which Robert Rogers was engaged at Merrimac, all the omens of the sky, from the St. Lawrence and Penobscot to the Niagara and Ohio, threatened another French war.[1]

In the spring of that year Duquesne had sent out from Montreal an expedition which by June had built forts at Presqu' Isle and Le Boeuf, and in August had occupied Venango, thus commanding the portages from Lake Erie to the Alleghany. Throughout the summer the Indians of the north-west—the Miami, Sauk, Potawatomi, Chippewa, and even some of the Iroquois—were submitting to the representatives of the French king with the most zealous protestations of fidelity, some even bringing in English scalps in earnest of their sincerity. Already Dinwiddie of Virginia had sent out troops to throw up a fort at the forks of the Ohio, and was laying those plans which, with the coming of autumn, were to introduce George Washington to the world. In the east preparations for war went as briskly on. During the summer of 1749 the first redoubts and palisades at Halifax, on the south coast of Acadia, had been erected, and the battalions of Louisbourg had marched in behind the ramparts of the most northern of English fortresses; and under more immediate indications of conflict nearly one-third of the French inhabitants of the land, pastoral and listless as they were, were emigrating to their brethren in the west.

At the same time, international discussions showed that

1. Francis Parkman, *Montcalm and Wolfe.* Boston, 1905, Frontenac Edition, II, chapters I-V.

the theoretical claims of the two peoples were irreconcilable. The French extremists claimed to the heads of the waterways emptying into the St. Lawrence, the Great Lakes, and the Ohio; the English extremists, basing their title upon the wide territory overrun by the Six Nations, would have confined their rivals, outside Louisiana, to their meagre settlements in Ontario and Quebec.

For the colony of New Hampshire the *avant*-couriers of war were, as usual, sporadic outbreaks of violence and discontent among the unruly Indians who occupied the hinterland between the settlements and Canada; and it was in the suppression of these eruptions that Rogers was first called into service. The northern colonies were not well prepared for the extremity that was upon them. As the Mohawk chief Hendrick told their governors at the Albany conference of 1759,[2] they had but to look about to see that their country was bare of fortifications. "It is but a step from Canada hither," he said, "and the French may come at any time and turn you out of doors. like men, they are fortifying everywhere. But you are like women, exposed and open, without fortifications."

As the fever and tension of war increased, the tribes' responsiveness to it kept pace. In December, 1752, the assembly of New Hampshire authorized the cutting of a road to the fertile Cohase Meadows,[3] one hundred miles up on the Connecticut; and the appearance in 1753 of a company of woodsmen and guards in that extreme region, surveying the proposed highway, threw the Indians of the St. Francis tribe into a state of restless uneasiness.[4] Although the scheme was not pushed, they at once began a course of depredations and raids. The spring of 1754 witnessed petty attacks upon Stevenstown, Conticook, and other townships north of Rumford, in such numbers that in early summer Governor Wentworth ordered out a company, under Colonel Blanchard, to patrol the upper reaches of the Merrimac. In this company Rogers enlisted on August 23, and

---

2. *New York Colonial Documents,* VI, 863.

3. *New Hampshire Province Papers,* VI, 198.

4. *New Hampshire Province Papers,* VI, 199.

served until September 21[5]———the third time, except for various brief periods of militia duty, that he had been in the military employ of the colony. He was a valued accession to the corps, for of the country over which Blanchard attempted to extend a fan-like grip he had a ready and intimate knowledge. He did not, however, see real action; although the pestering inroads of the Indians continued, Blanchard did not even come to a skirmish with them, and the penurious assembly forced the dissolution of the command within two months. He was therefore free during the autumn to return to his later harvest, or to whatever adventurous pursuits he chose.

But not for long. Some weeks he spent in rather desultory employment near Rumford, hunting, farming, and selling cattle, and then, in midwinter, as belligerent measures went on apace, found employment as an enlisting officer. On May 28, 1754, the troops of Washington, encountering in the valley of the Monongahela the courier party of Coulon de Jumonville, had received the order to fire, and so opened the Seven Years war. The news of Washington's surrender at Fort Necessity on July 4 thus found the troops of Carolina, Virginia, and New York all mobilizing for western campaigns, and the burgesses of Pennsylvania and Maryland granting to the common cause all that their poverty or parsimony would allow.[6]

New England had always suffered so much from French warparties that she was eager to accoutre herself for battle. Shirley of Massachusetts wrung a large grant of money from the General Court, marched himself to forestall French occupation of the Chaudiere, and despatched Captain Winslow to build two forts on the Kennebec. In New Hampshire Wentworth had already detached a troop to search for a French fort falsely rumoured to be under construction on the Connecticut. As the first snows fell, plans were being matured among the upper tier of colonies for a northern expedition, at first vaguely designated as "against Canada," but as the months went by clearly aimed against Crown Point, always a thorn in New England's side.

5. *New Hampshire Province Papers*, VI, 296. Potter, *Military History of New Hampshire*, I, 118.
6. Parkman, *Montcalm and Wolfe*, I, Chapter VI.

As an enlisting agent for this last army Rogers found remunerative employment, as well as an opportunity to provide a small future command for himself. We first hear of him in this connection in January, 1755, when, without stopping to get permission from Governor Wentworth, he accepted employment under Major Joseph Frye of Massachusetts to raise twenty men for the Bay Colony's quota.[7]

This occupation he was compelled to interrupt to extricate himself from grave legal difficulties. Early in February he was suspected of being implicated with others in counterfeiting the bills of credit of the provinces, a crime punishable according to the inhumane laws of the period, by an extreme penalty. On February 7th he was arrested and tried before the Inferior Court at Rumford, with fifteen others, and so much evidence was adduced against him that he was under bond of £500 before the Superior Court at Portsmouth on February 12th.[8]

It was established during Rogers' examination that, while he was hunting near Rumford the previous autumn, he had been approached by one Sullivan of Boston, a maker of counterfeit notes, who had offered to buy three yoke of oxen which Rogers kept for sale, and, showing him a handful of new bills, had given him one of twenty shillings for pasturing his horse. Hoping to get a large quantity of the counterfeit money, Rogers had brought his oxen to the place appointed, but had found that Sullivan, alarmed, was already fled from the country. Rogers testified also that he had asked Captain Blanchard and others to become partners with him in counterfeiting, "to find out if they were concerned in the matter;" and that they had refused and had warned him of the business in the strongest terms. Four of those who were tried with Rogers were sent to jail, and five others were admitted to bond.

He was badly frightened, and went at once to Portsmouth to find means of clearing himself;[9] meanwhile twenty-four men

7. *New Hampshire Province Papers,* VI, 364.

8. *New Hampshire Court Files,* Secretary of State's Office, No. 26954 and others.

9. In this matter of counterfeiting, see the papers used in the Inferior Court, Feb. 7th, 1754, and still preserved at Concord, New Hampshire. The bills counterfeited were of twenty, ten, and six shilling denominations. ((continued on next page)

whom he had enlisted for Massachusetts had gathered there, and a happy thought struck him. Finding that his own province was greatly in need of volunteers, and of capable enlisting officers to drum them up, he secured a commission from Wentworth himself, and the next day turned over all his soldiers to the New Hampshire government. When the hour set for his trial arrived a week later, he had so curried favour that he was admitted as king's evidence, and apparently escaped scot free.[10]

He returned up-country, and set about registering soldiers for Colonel Blanchard, who was to command the single regiment which the province was sending against Crown Point. Here he met with marked success, until Frye, with the backing of Shirley, complained to Wentworth of his conduct, stating that Rogers had secured his first volunteers by the use of king's money, and demanding that he be given exemplary punishment for treacherously and illegally returning them for New Hampshire. Wentworth, however, shielded his subordinate by replying that Frye's agreement with Rogers was utterly irregular, and that the latter, "whom I am told is recognized for a capital offense," was out of his reach.[11] Indeed, although in April fresh evidence against Rogers as a counterfeiter was produced by a farmer of Exeter, who had received bad notes from him, he was not further molested.[12]

The two Joseph Blanchards (one of whom Rogers had asked to join him), John Goffe, and Matthew Thornton were the justices who conducted the examination. The general impression to be gained from the answers of Rogers to their questions is that he had been temporarily led astray, in part by native dishonesty, in part by a rural want of judgment, but had early forsaken his evil course in alarm.

10. No Superior Court records of his trial have been preserved, and the sole statement upon which this explanation of his continued liberty is based (perhaps an insufficient one) is that in the *New Hampshire Province Papers*, VI, 364, in which Frye states that Rogers had gone to Portsmouth to take the steps suggested.

11. John Winslow, *Journal (Ms.)*, *Massachusetts Historical Society*, I, 9.

12. This farmer, named Carty Gilman, when searched as a suspect, had on his person two counterfeit bills and a letter from Rogers; the letter he stuffed in his mouth and partially ate before it could be recovered. The decipherable portion, still preserved, runs: "Mr. Gilman, for God's sake do the work that you promised me that you would do. By no means fail, or you will destroy me forever. Sir, my life lies at your providence; once more I adjure you by your Maker to do it, for why should such an honest man be killed?" Gilman confessed that he had received several bills from Captain Rogers, some of which he had passed, others of which he had returned.

The New Hampshire quota of five hundred men was now almost complete, and ready to march; the assembly, acting in unison with those of Massachusetts, Connecticut, and New York, had voted £30,000 toward the expense of the joint attack on Crown Point; and the state's experienced soldiers could not be kept waiting in the law-courts.

In Blanchard's regiment, Rogers, who had enlisted more men than any other agent, and who, as an old friend and subordinate of the commander, had given full proof of his merits as a fighter, was at the end of spring appointed captain of the first company.[13] His avenue to distinction was now fairly open.

The plan of the first campaign of the war General Braddock had determined upon two months previously, in conference with the governors of the colonies at Alexandria, Virginia. The commander-in-chief was himself to cross the Alleghanies and reduce Fort Duquesne; Governor Shirley of Massachusetts was to head an expedition against Fort Frontenac and Niagara on the Great Lakes; Moncton was to take ship against the French posts which threatened Nova Scotia; and Sir William Johnson, whom Admiral Sir Peter Warren had placed in charge of his extensive lands on the Mohawk years before, and who had just been made Indian superintendent, was to lead the long dreamed-of attack upon Crown Point. Thanks to the zeal of the northern colonies, when the last-named commander hastened back to Albany with Braddock's instructions, he found his forces everywhere mustering with arms and stores, and ready to begin their march. The troops were of heterogeneous origin.[14] Connecticut had voted twelve hundred men, Rhode Island four hundred, Massachusetts twelve hundred, New York eight hundred. In May and June, together with swarms of Mohawk Indians, they all began to converge toward their appointed camp at the "Flats" above Albany; and in the general movement the New Hampshire regiment at once entered upon its term of service. Rogers company was the earliest in motion.

The first instructions given to the regiment to march were

---

13. Potter, *Military History of New Hampshire*, I, 129.
14. Parkman, *Montcalm and Wolfe*, II, Chapters VII and IX.

blundering.[15] Ignorant, like all his counsellors, of the actual geography of the country about Lakes George and Champlain, Wentworth on May 28th announced his intention of sending the regiment against Crown Point by a shortcut through Cohase Meadows on the high Connecticut. A rendezvous was chosen on its banks some miles above Lancaster, and—so Wentworth thought—only four days across the wilds of Vermont from the English headquarters above Albany. Far from being expeditious, a route more roundabout, more exposed to attack, and more poorly calculated to assist the forward movement of Johnsons main force from the south, could scarcely have been chosen. Shirley immediately protested, but for the present the governor's instructions could only be obeyed. While the remainder of the troops were gathering at Canterbury, Rogers with his fifty men was sent on to Cohase, there to build a fort at the rendezvous. This rough rampart, thrown up during the month of June, he named Fort Wentworth, and after posting a sufficient guard behind its walls, at once returned south.[16] Meanwhile, Johnson had warned Wentworth early in June against going any farther northward; and the main column of provincials, already straggling through the forest to Stevenstown, was recalled to a secure line of march. On July 20th, Blanchard and his men set out along the proper route, by way of Charleston and Fort Dummer, and arrived on August 12th at Albany. The regiment rested a few days in town, and was then sent to guard the companies and wagons moving slowly up the Hudson to Fort Edward.

Here, at the end of three weeks, Rogers was given the employment in which he was to make his distinctive military mark, and for which his talents designed him. While Johnson's army, preceded by squadrons of axe-men hewing the

---

15. *New Hampshire Province Papers,* VI, 386, 392, and ff.

16. Rogers' *Journals* say: "Upon taking command of a company of the troops furnished by the province of New Hampshire, I made several excursions, pursuant to special orders from the governor, on the northern and western frontiers, with a view to deter the French and Indians from making inroads upon us by that way. In this manner I was employed until the month of July." (page viii). For an account of the fort Rogers built see Potter's *Military History of New Hampshire,* I, 144. Rogers was probably formally enlisted April 25th, 1755. *Idem,* p. 125.

way, pushed on to Lake George, Blanchard was ordered to defend Fort Edward, still incomplete; but the tall young captain was called in to an interview with the general, to whom he had been recommended as a person well acquainted with the haunts and passes of the enemy, and the Indian mode of righting. The shrewd, frank baronet was impressed with Rogers' presence and speech.[17] His army, for the most part a badly organized concourse of farmers and farmers' sons, pressing into a forest alive with French spies and hostile Indians, stood in dire need of a body of efficient scouts; and he saw his opportunity to use such a frontiersman to advantage.

The bold young provincial was therefore at once detached from Blanchard's command, and ordered, with a party of selected and hardy woodsmen, to hold himself in readiness for special ranging excursions. Within a few days he was sent away to follow and explore the upper distances of the Hudson, to the west of Lake George, and was therefore absent when, on September 8th, the French army which Dieskau had marched too rashly to the head of the lake was defeated, and its leader killed. This barren victory, closing for a moment major operations in that quarter, gave only a further impulse to Rogers' forays and scouts, for the defensive columns at Crown Point and Ticonderoga, settling pugnaciously down before William-Henry, the new fort on Lake George, required constant surveillance. Within a month he had proved his indispensability to Johnson, and as the colonial legions melted away to the proportions of a large garrison he was fairly divorced from the frontier settlement, with all its peaceful dangers to a nature like his, and devoted to the excur-

---

17. Rogers' *Journals,* page 8. Johnson wrote to Sir Charles Hardy: "Captain Rogers bravery and veracity stand very clear in my opinion, and that of all who know him. Though his regiment is gone he remains here a volunteer, and is the most active man in our army. Tomorrow he purposes to set out with two or three picked men to take a review of Ticonderoga, and proceed to Crown Point for a prisoner. I mention him particularly as I understand that some insinuations have been made to his disadvantage. I believe him to be as brave and as honest a man as any I have equal knowledge of, and both myself and the army are convinced he has distinguished himself since he has been among us, superior to most, inferior to none, of his rank." *Johnson Mss.,* 3, 83. (October 13th, 1755.)

sions and alarms of war. As the remaining battalions established themselves behind their new bulwarks, he found himself designated for the special services of irregular warfare, at first under the direct command of Johnson himself, later under the commissioners sent to the fort by the colonies.[18]

Indeed, the incidents of the first six months sufficed to establish Rogers' reputation and position.[19] Before. the close of 1755 had made seven sallies from Fort William-Henry, had mapped in detail the French works at Crown Point and Ticonderoga, had thoroughly explored the surrounding country, and had repeatedly taken prisoners whose examination yielded facts of the greatest value concerning the enemy's position. His squads, which numbered from four to fifty he handled, in Johnson's words, with "unparalleled boldness and usefulness." He was the eyes of the English camp.

In February and March of 1756 he continued his tactics with signal success, twice on bitterly cold nights marching sixty men within hailing-distance of the French forts, and setting in flames the villages under their very walls, In a winter noted for the general listlessness with which the war was conducted, his long expeditions furnished the only illumination on the page of affairs. The northern colonies, deeply interested in the reduction of Crown Point, were especially regardful of his services, and as the spring assemblies convened official notice was taken of his exploits. In late February the New York House granted him 125 Spanish milled pieces of eight "as a gratuity for his extraordinary courage, conduct and diligence against the French and their Indians."[20] A proposal for a similar measure was made in New Hampshire; while Shirley, quite forgetting his old score, twice urged the Massachusetts Court to show a like mark of their approbation.[21]

---

18. Potter, *Military History of New Hampshire*, I, 155. A council of war was held at Lake George in November, 1755, and by its decision Rogers and his company were among those retained at Fort William-Henry as a garrison throughout the winter. He represented all the colonies, and not New Hampshire in particular—a fact which later caused him endless difficulty in securing his own and his men's pay.
19. Rogers' *Journals*, pages 1-12.
20. *Massachusetts Archives*, IV, 546. This was on February 25, 1756.
21. *Massachusetts Archives*, CIX, 243.

Upon their refusal, Shirley resolved with customary zeal to take some step which would ensure Rogers continuance in his present station, and increase the scope of his possibilities for service, and in March sent for him to come to Boston. In the council chamber of the old Province House the governor gave the young officer a commission as captain of an independent company of rangers. Specific directions to enlist woodsmen accustomed to travelling and hunting, and to use them in harassing the French, accompanied the commission.[22]

Within a fortnight Rogers had attracted to his standard the requisite number of tried frontiersmen, and, sending a party with his brother Richard to Albany, marched with the rest across the forest-covered hills of lower Vermont. The manner of his arrival was characteristic.[23] Emerging on a bright May morning from the woods near the enemy's post, he lay in wait opposite, hoping some party might venture across to be attacked. In the afternoon and evening four or five hundred gaily-uniformed volunteers, piloted by Indians in war-paint, paddled loiteringly past; but although the English kept their posts till ten o'clock next day, they found no opportunity to ambush them. At that hour they discovered a herd of cattle grazing close behind them, and shot more than a score, whose tongues they found "a great refreshment." The reports of their guns, unfortunately, were heard by the French, and eleven canoes of armed men crossed the lake so directly and threateningly toward them that they were forced to disperse to escape their pursuers. Later they passed down the lake on a raft, seeing as they did so the French soldiery drawn up on glittering parade, with a crowd of interested savages watching them, beside the "old carrying-place" of Ticonderoga.

Beginning with October, 1755, and continuing nearly six years, all Rogers expeditions, adventures, and exploits, are recorded in his journals;—dryly, unambitiously, but with a detail that in spite of itself glows at some passages into vividness. The forces he commanded, and the magnitude of the operations in which he engaged, grew from a small beginning until he was among

22. Rogers' *Journals*, pages 13, 14, 15.
23. Rogers' *Journals*, pages 16, 17.

the most renowned and efficient of provincial commanders; but the spectacular zest, the bold dash, of his achievement was always the same. No branch of American arms of the period was so glamorously adventurous, so active, dangerous, and fascinating; none balanced so well the unique piquancy of forest campaigning against its constant perils and privations. The first four weary years that the campaign dragged on about Crown Point were emblazoned by his feats alone. With headquarters at William-Henry, his command held in leash all the debatable ground that lay to the north, and ranged over plain and valley to give battle or secure information. The two attractive lakes, George and Champlain, with the hills, the deep woods, the brooks and ponds that environed them, were in all seasons and weathers their constant arena, and a home of wonderful variety and charm. In summer they made their daring dashes upon the placid water which for miles mirrored back the surrounding rock and mountain, paddling their canoes noiselessly along shores whose drooping foliage made for them an embowered lane, and slipping past islands asleep in August haze, in a silence broken only by the screaming of the jay, or the soughing of the wind through the sumac and ivy. In frozen winter, they would break a midnight camp as the rising moon threw its chill reflection over the glittering waste of the forest, or under a wan and dying sun thread their way on snowshoes along some ice-bound stream, under birches and alders stooping with their feathery burden. The fascination of the surprise, of the sharp report that rang over the sleeping hill, of the gloomy ambush and the breathless pursuit or flight, was stronger with them than the fear of death, or the longing for security and peace. From spring till autumn contact with nature filled them with hardy energy. Nor were their services ever insignificant. With their increasing strength and prestige they kept the whole region, and every French or Indian encampment, under continuous survey. They reconnoitred their forts, took prisoners to extort information, intercepted provisions, fired grain-ricks and houses, killed cattle, captured *bateaux*, and reported the most trivial movements of troops. Their vigilance and pugnacity kept them always penetrating the enemy's lines, stealing upon his entrenchments and sentries,[24] engaging his outparties in hornet-like skirmishes, and retiring with volleys into the darkness of an unforeseen ambuscade.

Rogers' command was steadily augmented. On July 20, 1756, he was given a second company, captained by his brother Richard, and in the next month thirty Stockbridge Indians were placed under his direction, to serve upon missions which required endurance and sly daring rather than calm judgment; while during the late autumn, two new companies, under Captain Spikeman and Hobbs, were ordered up to spend the winter at William-Henry. In one of these Robert's brother James was ensign. With the full advent of spring two more companies were raised, one from the Jerseys under Captain Burgin, the other from inactive regiments of English regulars. Still another was afterwards added, so that during the greater portion of the three years' campaigning about Crown Point which followed 1756, Rogers commanded seven or eight companies, the whole forming a perfectly unified and coherent battalion, although its various parts were often dispersed on widely different errands. His comprehensive authority over the body was recognized early in 1758, when Abercrombie appointed him a major commanding all the rangers in His Majesty's service. Thenceforth he directed the movement of the whole corps, retaining, however, command of an especial company with which he himself undertook the most dangerous and onerous expeditions. With him or under him, at different times, such famous and capable soldiers as John Stark, Israel Putnam, and James Dalyell served their apprenticeship.

These rangers stand among the most picturesque of all the troops which have served on the American continent, for both temper and appearance answered well to their rough and audacious life. Most of them were the resolute sons of the border

---

24. For this and whatever matter is not hereafter specifically credited to another source, see Rogers *Journals*, London, 1765. For the account of the habits of Rogers' men and their method of fighting, material has been drawn in especial from the plan of discipline which he drew up for his regular companies in 1757.

villages and farms, inured, like their commander, to the fatigues of harassing and unbelievable journeys, the extremes of heat and cold, and distressing privations of food and shelter during long periods; fearless, steady of nerve, and resourceful of mind. A few were true Puritans; some others, worse than Rogers, added to a stern forcefulness characteristics by no means so praiseworthy, and were rough and drunken when off duty, unscrupulous in private morals, and cruel in battle. In active campaigning, withal, they were brave, orderly, and efficient. There was the same, want of smooth coordination between their loose private life and their hard fighting capacity that marked the buccaneers of Drake and Hawkins. They wore a uniform which varied slightly in the different companies, but which in all was only a military variation of the ordinary garb of hunter and trapper; and each carried a smooth-bore firelock, with sixty rounds of powder and ball, and a heavy hatchet. Their life in the field was one of infinite vigilance and hourly readiness for action. Except upon marshy ground, they marched in single file, far enough apart that one shot might not kill two men, and with a cloud of skirmishers to the front and sides.

The usual fords and paths they carefully avoided, and in passing along a large body of water, kept at such a distance that no hostile ambuscade could cut off their retreat. At every suspicious thicket and hedgy bank they stopped to reconnoitre. Any considerable force of the enemy was from behind logs and the heavy covert of shrubs and bushes; and when overwhelmed, in numbers the rangers retired with a slow, enchafing fire until they reached a defensible eminence. Their aim would check a blackbird's swift flight in mid-air, or bring down a chattering squirrel as it ran along the topmost branch of an oak. When encamped for the night, they posted their sentries in silent groups of six, two of whom were constantly alert, so as to avoid the necessity of relief from the main body. At dawn, the hour of stealthy Indian attacks, they were always awake and in position to repel a surprise. Some of their forced marches were almost incredible. In midwinter they would skate down the sheeted lakes, and in summer send their light canoes shooting over their smooth surface, always hugging the shore, and moving preferably by night to avoid detection. To surprise and thwart the enemy was their eternal ambition. And of this rough and stalwart crew Rogers, with his commanding physique, his undying energy and powers of woodland leadership, his ready wit and rollicking bonhomie, was the heart and informing spirit.

Out of the almost monotonous succession of raids, skirmishes, captures of prisoners, and spying trips of the rangers, two principal engagements stand forth in relief. The first occurred in January, 1757, soon after the arrival of Abercrombie and Loudon with the whole army of the centre at Fort Edward.[25]

On the seventh of the month Rogers took seventy-five men, among them Lieutenant John Stark, and skated down the lake, frozen deep and wind-swept of the heavy snow, until finally he turned to the north-west and entered the woods. His soldiers had provided themselves with snowshoes, and with these they pushed on northward, now tacking to the east, now to the west, but keeping always several miles to the left of the glittering waste of Lake George and Lake Champlain, and moving single file over iron-bound swamps, ice-clad rocks, through thickets drifted high with snow and under firs and pines bowed with an icy weight. At night they bivouacked in the lee of a tall hill, scraping back the snow from a projecting bank, and throwing down their beds of spruce and pine bough about a blazing campfire. The morning of the twenty-first, dawning with a cold rain which multiplied the exertions and discomfort of their travel, discovered them breaking camp in the deep woods halfway between Crown Point and Ticonderoga. The gusts and flaws of the unseasonable day increased. Shielding their guns as best they could from the dripping branches, and plunging at every step into the deep slush

25. *Journals*, p. 38 ff. Parkman, *Montcalm and Wolfe*, II, 129. Potter, *Military History of New Hampshire*, I, 160 ff. The valley between Crown Point and Ticonderoga is less than five miles in breadth and some seventeen or eighteen long. From the beginning of the campaigns about the two lakes, it was guarded by four distinct outposts of the French, and constantly ranged over by swarms of Indians, and a force of Canadian partisans under their own bold colonial leader, Marin.

of the forest glades, they marched eastward toward the guiding bosom of Lake Champlain, three miles away. As they drew near the edge of the ice, they discovered a sledge, drawn by a team of heavy Norman horses, emerging from a neighbouring headland, and obviously bound from Ticonderoga to Crown Point. At once Rogers dispatches Stark along the bank to cut off its progress, and himself prepared to sally out to intercept it in the rear. But even as he watched, eight or ten more sleds emerged from cover, and pursued the track of the first. In hot haste he sent a messenger to warn his lieutenant not to show himself, but it was too late. Already Stark was upon the ice, and the whole train had taken alarm and turned in galloping flight back toward Ticonderoga.

By a quick pursuit the rangers captured three of the sledges with seven men, but the rest, with their drivers and guards, escaped. The prisoners were Languedoc Frenchmen, and when interrogated, revealed an alarming state of affairs. At Ticonderoga there lay between the rangers and Fort William-Henry— besides three hundred and fifty regular troops—three hundred fresh Canadians and Indians, spoiling for a fight, and prepared to march upon an instant's notice. Rogers perceived that the fugitives would give the alarm within the hour, and that only decisive measures and the best of luck could save his command from total extinction.

He instantly ordered his men to return on the double-quick to their bivouac of the previous night, and there rekindle their fires to dry their guns for battle. Midday was past before they had completed this operation, and they at once set out southward, pushing their way through the dripping foliage, over snowy, broken ground. In this manner they advanced half a mile, and then commenced the ascent of a steep hill, even more densely wooded than its neighbours. As their foremost men were but five yards from the summit, a furious volley blazed forth from the guns of more than two hundred of the enemy, arranged in a semi-circle along the ridge above. Two men were killed on the spot and others wounded; among the latter Rogers himself, whose scalp was grazed by a bullet. The rangers, immediately returning the fire, gave way in some disorder, and were hotly pursued by the enemy to the opposite crest. Here they made a stubborn stand, finally beating back their assailants for the moment, and gaining time to ensconce themselves for a determined resistance. Twice the Canadians attempted to dislodge them by a flank attack, and repeatedly they advanced in force from the front; but having the advantage of the ground, and sheltered by large trees, the English stood firm and did heavy execution. As the drizzly afternoon closed in an early dusk, Rogers received a ball through his hand and wrist. One of the lieutenants bound the wound with the ribbon of his queue, however, and the captain, although disabled from loading his gun, continued to encourage his men. The French tried threats and cajolery, as well as force, to persuade the English to surrender, and calling Rogers by name, repeatedly gave him "the strongest assurances of their esteem and friendship." A constant fire was nevertheless maintained until darkness shut down, when the rangers were enabled to creep away, and furtively make off homeward.[26] They had lost fourteen killed, and twelve wounded or missing, but had inflicted far more serious injury upon the French.

It was this smart little battle, capping so bold and creditable a dash, that first really spread abroad the reputation of Rogers. The commander-in-chief, Abercrombie, sent him his especial thanks, and strongly commended his merits to Lord Loudon. Abercrombie's nephew, who had accompanied Rogers upon a short expedition, and apparently conceived a personal esteem for him, wrote him from Albany that "you cannot imagine how all ranks of people here are pleased with your conduct and your

---

26. Captain Spikeman was killed in this action, and it is stated by Caleb Stark (*Memoir of General John Stark*, Concord, 1860.) that Rogers was twice wounded. He also gives (p. 18) the story of the heroic retreat. "By marching all night, they reached Lake George at eight o'clock next morning. The wounded, who, during the march, had kept up their spirits, were by that time so overcome with cold, fatigue, and loss of blood that they could march no farther. It became, therefore, necessary to forward a notice to the fort, that sleighs might be sent for them. Lieut. Stark volunteered for this purpose, and, by undergoing extraordinary fatigues, reached Fort William-Henry, distant forty miles, the next evening."

men's behaviour." Every newsletter of the time mentioned the affair with commendation, and coupled with accounts of his former dashes, the story went east and west.

The second engagement, which occurred more than a year after, did not have so happy an issue. For some months Rogers had been confined to the fort by his wound and by an attack, of the smallpox, a general epidemic of which more than deci-mated his troops, and carried off his brother Richaed. He was then marched to Albany, and embarked for Halifax, where—until the expedition then on foot against Louisbourg was abandoned—his forces were broken into scouting columns, gangs of haymakers, and press-gangs in pursuit of deserters. In early autumn he and his depleted companies were remanded to Fort Edward, for William-Henry had been captured and destroyed during his absence by Montcalm. He was engaged during the winter in training fresh recruits, and no notewor-thy expedition took place until March, 1758. On March 10th, however, he was ordered to Ticonderoga, with but 180 men, although he had asked for more and considered double the number necessary. The French fort at this moment contained four hundred regular soldiers, while near it lay a large body of Indians and Canadians; and through the recent escape of a deserter to their ranks, the enemy were upon the *qui vive* for Rogers' approach. For two days his men streamed silently through the frozen forest, over several feet of snow, and by the night of the eleventh were upon the narrows of Lake George. Here they bivouacked, keeping sentries far out through the gloom of the woods, and patrolling the neighbouring portions of the lake. The next day they pushed on upon skates, alarmed once by a dog trotting far out upon the ice, and again near dusk. by some phosphorescent patches of rotten wood on the shore, which they mistook for hostile campfires. On the thir-teenth they found themselves in territory distinctly French, and exchanged the cold lake for the secret, hushed heart of the wilderness. Travelling upon snowshoes, they kept on along the crest of a line of which overlooked the advanced camps of the main French army at Ticonderoga, and by noon had reached a point west of Bald Mountain, near the bold promontory now called Rogers' Rock. Here they refreshed themselves until three, and then again set off over ground so rough and rocky that for ease in walking they kept near the bed of a small rivulet. To the right rose the steep promontory that overlooked the lake, and all about the naked, icy waste, the tops of the highest bushes peeping from beneath four feet of snow.

Within an hour the advance guard came running back with the information that a hundred Indians were approaching upon the ice of the brook. Rogers immediately drew up his men under cover, their guns commanding the bed of the stream, and their backs to the hill; and when the foremost rank of the incautious enemy arrived opposite his centre, gave the order to fire. Half the Indians were killed on the spot, and as the rest fled in confusion, Rogers, believing this troop their main body, gave the order for a pursuit. He was rudely surprised. As the dashing rangers poured along the stream they were met by a fresh array of several hundred more Canadians and savages, with some French officers commanding. Fifty of the English were shot down, and the rest driven back in disorder, a yelling, firing mob at their heels. With his accustomed expedition Rogers rallied his men, and formed them upon the steep slope to their right. Twice he repulsed his assailants with severe loss, and twice they returned to the attack, reducing each time the number of defenders. The third assault continued for an hour and a half, during which time the commixed enemy were never twenty yards from the rangers, and often intermingled with them and fought hand to hand. Until near sunset the uproar of firing and war-whoops continued, by which time more than a hundred of Rogers' men lay dead or badly wounded in the snow, and a flanking guard, which he had stationed on a neighbouring hill, had surrendered. The Indians were on the point of gaining the heights in the rear, and as the sun sank Rogers, with twenty survivors, made up the steep and escaped to the south-east. Tradition relates that the chagrined commander, having fallen behind his men to fire a parting shot, escaped only by reversing his snowshoes and sliding down the steep descent of the mountain five hundred feet to the lake; and that the Indians, considering this wonderful feat significant of the interposition of the Great Spirit, at once gave up further pursuit.

In this fight, Rogers lost 130 of his 180 men; none of the wounded escaped, for the savages either despatched them on the spot, or left them to perish from exposure. He states that for his part he killed 150 and wounded as many more; but at best the action was but a sorry affair for the English. The major was inclined to place the blame for the "unfortunate scout" upon the shoulders of Colonel Haviland, who, "doubtless with reason, doubtless with ability to vindicate his conduct," sent him forth with such an "incomprehensibly reduced party. What we should have done had we been 400 or more strong I will not pretend to determine," he concludes his account of the defeat. There can be but little doubt that Haviland erred in allowing him so small a command, and that thereby he was responsible in major part for the disaster; but even Rogers' account does not attempt to disguise the fact that for once, at the moment of the attack, he was wanting in judgment and caution.

Lesser incidents indicative of the daring impassivity of the rangers in the face of danger, of their uncomplaining endurance of extreme hardship, and of other characteristics reaching from the merely picturesque to the grimly or naively humorous, lie thickly sown through the pages of the *Journals*. To enumerate them would be impossible. Such words as these taken from the very first pages of Rogers' record, may well represent a whole chapter of suffering and weariness.

> We approached very near their fort by night, and were driven by the cold (now very severe) to take shelter in one of their evacuated huts; before day there was a fall of snow which obliged us, with all possible speed, to march homeward. After being almost exhausted with hunger, cold, and fatigue, we had the good fortune to kill two deer for refreshment.

In March, 1759, during a period of excessive cold, twenty-three of Rogers' scouts were frostbitten and were perforce sent back exhausted, "under the charge of a careful sergeant;" but the main body, almost overcome at times, pushed on, two thirds of them with frozen feet, till the object of their expedition was attained. Again and again they slept unprotected in the most inclement weather, forbidden by caution to kindle a fire, by expediency in marching to carry blankets. Twice during his campaigns his men were overtaken upon Champlain by sudden squalls, and once a single craft was overturned and its occupants drowned. Scarcely one of his scores of raids was performed without fatigue, pain, and loss of life, and, often as his achievements were spectacular, still oftener they were the result merely of obscure, persevering labour, and were bought by a triumph over difficulties which less hardened soldiers would have deemed insuperable. Some of the more notable events cannot be omitted. On October 21st, 1755, Rogers and his squad lay all night within three hundred yards of Crown Point; and at daybreak, as the bugles blew from the parapets, he advanced alone much nearer, wriggling along behind fresh bushes which he held upright in his hands. So many soldiers came out that he lay as if petrified, until one approached so near that he had to kill him with his fusee, and hurriedly dash back into the forest. In October, 1757, he tried to take a prisoner near Ticonderoga, but unsuccessfully; until he marched his men boldly down the fort's road upon a sentry, hailed him in French, and spirited him away, "cutting his breeches and coat from him that he might march, with the greater ease and expedition." In midsummer of 1756, again, on nights all too moonlit and calm for his purpose, he took fifty men in five whaleboats down Lake Champlain, and passed with muffled oars under the very walls of Ticonderoga and Crown Point, so close that they heard the voices of the sentinel calling the watchword. During the day they lurked beneath drooping branches in the shadow of the shore, with *bateaux* passing and repassing on the hot, gleaming expanse, and even landing noisily near them. When the whaleboats, abandoned later in the year, were discovered at the head of Lake Champlain, Bougainville, the astounded French commander, propounded five different hypotheses for their being there. It was this same party who in June boarded and captured a schooner of forty tons bound for Canada, guarded by two lighters; and as Rogers honestly confesses, "we sunk and destroyed their vessels and cargoes, which consisted chiefly of wheat and flour, wine and brandy; some few casks of the latter we carefully concealed."

In the closing years of the war, Rogers and his now large command played a not insignificant part.[27] Early in 1758 Loudon was succeeded by Abercrombie, and the final active campaigns were set on foot. By the end of July the fortress of Louisbourg was in the hands of the English; by the end of August, Fort Frontenac; by the end of November, Fort Duquesne. Meanwhile Abercrombie at Fort Edward had ordered Rogers to muster his eight companies before June 10th, and was himself engaged in bringing his whole army up to Lake George. By June 28th he and Lord Howe had 16,000 men encamped upon the site of Fort William-Henry, and on July 5th embarked them in *bateaux* for Ticonderoga. Rogers had spent the preceding month, with fifty rangers, in scouting over the ground which the new movement was intended to conquer; and at the moment of embarkation he had secured complete new plans of the fort and the Indian encampment at Ticonderoga, and maps of the country at the foot of Lake George and the head of Lake Champlain, with the intervening portage.

When the army moved forward toward the most important grapple of the year, one which was expected to crush the French centre and destroy Montcalm's main force, he had his six hundred men all in readiness. In Abercrombie's advance, his ill-judged and disastrous attack upon Montcalm's strongly entrenched position, and his humiliating retreat, Rogers' corps held a prominent and honourable position. Like many others, the young major has left his testimony to the bravery of the scene as, on a fair July morning, with music, flags, the glitter of

---

27. Rogers, *Journals*, also available in a Leonaur edition.

arms, the parade of bright uniforms, and the flash of oars, the whole army moved down the sparkling, mountain-circled breast of Lake George. His corps held its place on the left of the army throughout the day and night, and when early in the morning the flotilla reached a point near the foot of the lake, he and Howe went on together to reconnoitre a landing.

When the army had been safely disembarked, and had commenced its march toward the head of Lake Champlain, his rangers again constituted the advance guard, leading the way through the mazes of the forest; and as such they aided in the destruction of a venturesome squadron of the French, which, after killing Lord Howe, had been caught between the leading columns of the English army. The next day Abercrombie pushed steadily on toward the head of Lake Champlain, where lay the main army of the enemy, only 3500 strong.

On the morrow, July eighth, Rogers was ordered at sunrise to beat the. French within the breastworks and *abattis* which Montcalm had thrown up across the rocky promontory of Ticonderoga.

> The line followed the top of a ridge, along which it zigzagged in such a manner that the whole front could be swept by flank-fires of musketry and grape. From its central part the ground sloped away like a natural glacis; while at the sides it was undulating and broken. Over this whole space, to the distance of a musket-shot from the works, the forest was cut down, and the trees left lying where they fell, with tops turned outward, forming one vast *abattis*, like a forest laid flat by a hurricane. But the most formidable obstruction was immediately along the front of the breastwork, where the ground was covered with heavy boughs overlapping and interlaced, with sharpened points bristling into the face of the assailants like the quills of a porcupine.[28]

It was behind these works that Rogers, with the assistance of several provincial regiments, drove the French pickets; his men

---

28. Parkman, *Montcalm and Wolfe*, II, 306.

and the other colonials then lay down in detachments, through the intervals between which the regulars advanced stolidly to the assault. Beyond all doubt it was fortunate for him that, having opened that hopeless charge, he was forced to lie and watch the ranks of his compatriots shattered and swept away by the withering fire the French poured into the military clearing. The full body of the British grenadiers was sent forward to storm the impregnable works before the provincials were allowed to support them; and not for a full hour could he have entered the tangled arena swept by the bullets of the enemy. Of his part in the dreadful carnage of the later afternoon we know little. "We toiled with repeated attacks for four hours,"[29] he writes, and there is no reason to doubt that his men, like some of their provincial comrades, found their way to the very foot of the *abattis*. When at seven o'clock the battle closed and retreat was ordered, the general directed him to bring up the rear as the broken army fell back to its starting-point below Lake George.

Within two days of the battle Rogers' ranging service commenced afresh, for his defeated commander was anxious to learn the state in which Montcalm's army lay at the opposite end of the lake; after a time, moreover, it became necessary to check the war parties which the French were constantly sending out to harass Abercrombie's communications with Fort Edward.[30] A Canadian partisan corps, organized by Marin in imitation of the rangers, was especially active, and in two excursions within ten days killed 150 English soldiers engaged in convoying wagons through the woods. Enraged at the repetition of these attacks, Abercrombie sent off Rogers with his rangers, Israel Putnam with-some provincials, and Captain Dalyell with a number of regulars, in pursuit toward the eastern extremity of Lake Champlain. For eight days they explored the basking August woods unsuccessfully; until in their return, having passed the night on the high cleared land where stood old Fort Anne, a crumbling survival of former wars, they prepared in the morning to strike camp and march in home.

---

29. Rogers, *Journals*, also available in a Leonaur edition.
30. Rogers, *Journal*, also available in a Leonaur edition.

They were south and east of the main English force, and in their whole recent march had seen no signs of the proximity of French or Indians; so that, forgetting the caution which had heretofore led him to enjoin the strictest silence upon his men, Rogers banteringly challenged Putnam to a contest of marksmanship, and cut a rude bullseye upon a neighbouring tree. Marin's corps of Canadians and Indians heard the shots, and at once took steps to surprise their reckless enemies. A thick-starting, heavily tangled and interlaced growth of shrubbery covered the long glacis about the old fort, and was penetrated only by a winding, gently sloping path. As the mixed English columns of scouts, regulars, and provincials issued in single file down this still dewy lane and out into the forest beyond, they were met by the concentrated fire of 500 men, lying in a semicircle about its head. For a moment all was confusion; Putnam, leading the men, was jerked into the lines of the enemy and taken prisoner; the advance guard, left without a commander, first recoiled upon itself and then dropped behind bushes to answer with a weak, scattering fire. Rogers and Dalyell, in the extreme rear, struggled hurriedly forward through the brush to rally their men; and before the sun had mounted a half-hour had them replying spiritedly and steadily to their opponents.

Four of Marin's successive attacks were repulsed, and in an hour his ranks were so broken that he was glad to allow his men to scatter back into the forest. After burying his own dead, Rogers pursued his way unmolested to Fort Edward. He was universally praised for his coolness and bravery, and a week later the general-in-chief, anxious to report even small successes, wrote to Pitt that "Rogers deserves much to be commended." The engagement was widely reported in colonial gazettes and newspapers.

In the final successful movements of the next year against Crown Point, Ticonderoga, and Montreal, Rogers assumed only the role of commander of an advance guard and force of picket-scouts. In June and July of 1759, Gage and Amherst, the latter the new commander-in-chief, moved down Lake George with a force so strong that it required all the ranger's 700 men to serve as a screen, and as guides through the various forest roads. In besieging Ticonderoga Amherst drew a lesson from Abercrombie's failure of the preceding year, and brought up his heavy cannon to blow its protecting redoubts to pieces. On the night of July 22nd the French, preparing to evacuate their indefensible position, left a match burning in the magazine, and took, to their boats with all their stores. At this hour Rogers happened to have sixty of his rangers in three *bateaux* upon the lake, where his men were making a nocturnal attempt to saw through a boom of timbers which had been thrown out below the fort, and which prevented the English boats from passing by to cut off the French retreat. He had scarce reached the boom when, with a loud reverberation, the soft summer night was lit up by the flaring explosion of the fort's magazine. Hastily he drew his boats alongside the-floating timbers, and opened fire upon the enemy, with such successes to drive ten of their most heavily laden craft ashore.[31] Three days later a party of his scouts brought back. news of the desertion and dismantling of Crown Point.

Two main services of the war remained to be performed by Rogers—the destruction of the St. Francis Indians and the reception of the surrender of the western posts. For the first the whole frontier breathed its relieved thanks. During three quarters of a century the Abenaki, Pennacook, and shreds of other tribes which dwelt near the junction of the St. Francis and St. Lawrence, Catholic but still savage, had been the scourge of the New England border. Rogers as a boy had known the horror of their raids, for it was one of their parties which had burned his father's home; and now, partly by reason of the long hatred of the colonists for them, partly for their recent violation of the rights of a party of truce, they were singled out to feel the specific anger of the victorious British.[32] In September Amherst gave Rogers two hundred men, and ordered him to "take revenge for the infamous cru-

---

31. Rogers, *Journal*, also available in a Leonaur edition.
32. Rogers, *Journal*, also available in a Leonaur edition.

elties and barbarities of the Indian scoundrels;" a command which he prepared to obey with the more alacrity that to his "own knowledge, in six years time they had carried into captivity and murdered 400 persons."

In whaleboats he slipped down Lake Champlain to its north end, eluding the French sloops still patrolling those waters, and hiding his craft in Missiquoi Bay, where he left two friendly Indians to guard them, struck out on the long overland journey toward St. Francis. On the evening of the second day the two Indians ran panting into camp with the startling news that four hundred French had discovered his boats and were in ardent pursuit. His party's retreat by water was cut off, all their provisions lost, and they were faced by the fearful certainty that other alarmed bands and troops would at once be out to intercept their path. With characteristic decision Rogers cut the knot of his difficulties, and determined to outmarch his pursuers, destroy the village before help could arrive, and return south by a hasty dash to Cohase Intervales and a voyage down the Connecticut. Accordingly he despatched an officer back through the forest to Crown Point to ask Amherst to send a relief party up the river to meet him, and set out northeast by forced marches. The way for the most part traversed limitless spruce swamps, so wet that his men splashed for hour after hour through a foot of water, and that to snatch a few hours sleep at night they had to lie among the tops of hastily felled trees; but for nine days they hurried on with almost delirious energy. At the end of that time, fording the swift, deep St. Francis river with the greatest peril, they found themselves within a few miles of the town. As dusk fell Rogers watched its darkening streets from a treetop, and later crept to its borders upon his hands and knees, finding the unsuspecting savages deep in the celebration of a marriage with dancing and feasting. In the dark hours immediately preceding dawn the next day his men took the village completely by surprise. With a fury fed by the sight of six hundred English scalps festooning the doorways of the houses, they killed the two hundred warriors of the place, drove the women and children into the woods, and burned everything except three granaries of maize. Five white captives were retaken.

Post-haste now Rogers set out for the Connecticut; for having examined several prisoners while his men, were loading themselves with such provisions as the smoking ruins afforded, he learned that the two large bodies of French and Indians were lying in wait for him nearby, still uncertain of his movements. The return trip was a sustained nightmare. For eight days he hurried his men up the St. Francis, past its headwaters, and on to Lake Memphremagog. Here their carefully husbanded supply of food was utterly exhausted, and that they might better subsist on the country through which they passed, he separated his men into small detachments. Within two days some of his force were shot by the pursuing Canadians, while the rest, killing an occasional squirrel or partridge, or living: on groundnuts or lily-roots, toiled on toward the Connecticut. The French still hung upon their rear, slaying and capturing in all fifty men. The members of two of the bands, almost insane from hunger, fell upon the bodies of their comrades and ate them. Those that finally reached the Connecticut, however, were followed no more, and, gathering again in a single party, dizzy with weakness, struggled on down its banks to the mouth of the Amonsook. Here they looked confidently for the succour and provisions for which Rogers had sent to Amherst; but they were rudely disappointed. The forest glades were empty, except for a fresh fire burning brightly amid the signs of a recent camp; their comrades had come, had waited, and were just gone. Rogers says:

> Our distress, our grief and consternation, were truly inexpressible. After so many days weary march over steep, rocky mountains, or through wet, dirty swamps—after such expectation that we should find our distresses alleviated—our spirits, entirely sank within us, for we saw no hope that we should escape a miserable death by famine.

His own indomitable energy alone remained unshaken, and with two of his strongest comrades he made a raft and pushed on, engaging to return help within ten days. The current carried them down with perilous swiftness, and they tried to steady their wretched craft with branches of trees improvised as paddles. When it was finally lost over White River Falls, the requisite distance but half covered, they were too weak to wield the axe in constructing another, and so burnt trees down and to the proper length, lashing the logs together with grapevine. A day later they again approached the roar of a waterfall—this time the Watttockquitchey; the desperate Rogers went below, swam into the rapids, and caught the second precious raft as it came over, for they were too far spent to build a third. By great good fortune they next day killed a partridge, and, thus strengthened, finally reached the first military post on that long, lonely river, and sent back aid to their starving friends.

In Amherst's final summer advance upon Montreal from Crown Point, Rogers participated, first scouting over the country to glean general information, and later, in an unsuccessful attempt to surprise St. John's, a small fort just above the foot of Lake Champlain, taking the minor post of St. d'Estrese in the same valley. The enemy were carting hay here into the stockade, and—watching their opportunity—his men dashed from the woods and followed one of the loads through before the heavy gate could be closed. Later he was with Haviland, and in command of his full corps of 600, when the evacuation of Isle aux Noix was forced, and having later been sent to subdue the valley of the Sorrel, returned in time to witness the surrender of Montreal, September 8th, 1760. His services during these final months carried him over several hundred miles of territory, and twice won for him stray words of commendation from Amherst.

On September 12th the commander-in-chief did him the honour of designating him as the officer who should receive the surrender of all the French posts along the Great Lakes, an arduous task which, while involving no real responsibility, was distinguished in that it elevated him to an office ambassadorial in nature. With two hundred troops he set out on the thirteenth, and, despite the obstacles presented by great distance, rough roads, and bad weather, had accomplished his duties by December first, receiving a reluctant submission at Detroit and Shawneetown, visiting Niagara, Fort de Boeuf, Presqu' Isle, Venango, and Pittsburg, apprising the hostile Indian tribes of the issue of the conflict, and everywhere forcing upon the unwilling French inhabitants the oath of allegiance. The larger part of his journey was performed in whaleboats, with which he ascended the St. Lawrence, passed by Niagara Falls, and skirted the southern shores of Lake Ontario, while a detachment drove cattle for provisions along the forested bank. A projected expedition from Detroit to Mackinaw failed because of stormy winds and the piling up of ice-cakes on Lake Huron. The fertile and varied landscape of the regions through which he passed was a source of never-ending interest to the major; and at one point in his journey, near Presqu' Isle, he met the chief Pontiac—of whom more anon.

CHAPTER 3

The Cherokee War &
Pontiac's Rebellion

On February 14th, 1761, Rogers arrived alone at New
York, having travelled from Detroit to Pittsburg through the
rich, trackless forest of Ohio and eastern Pennsylvania, following the shores of Lake Sandusky and Erie, and descending
the Muskingum River, stopping at many Indian villages—
Wyandotte, Iroquois, and Delaware—along the way; and proceeding from Pittsburg to Philadelphia by way of the common road. He records that he was greatly fatigued when he
reached Manhattan Island, for he had travelled almost continuously since his departure from Montreal the preceding fall,
sometimes covering twenty miles of rough, heavily timbered
country, or paddling over a great extent of stormy water, between sunrise and dusk.[1] His duty was done, however, and,
having reported the fulfilment of his mission at headquarters, he obtained an indeterminate furlough, without either
surrendering his commission or losing his liability to active
service. He was complimented by the general upon his ability
and performances, and received the indirect praise conveyed
by instructions to keep ever within call, lest his services as a
border commander should be required.[2]

The hour was a bright one for the major. He was not yet
thirty years old; he had risen against many obstacles of birth

1. Rogers, *Journal*, also available in a Leonaur edition.
2. *Dartmouth Mss.*, Rogers to the King, March 13, 1775.

and education to a position of real command in a distinct and spectacular arm of the service, and had impressed his superiors, not merely American but English, with his trustworthiness and brilliancy in that arm; his fame had gone abroad through all the provinces as a dashing, bold, and experienced fighter. He had the consciousness that, as he himself boasted, no one of his rank "had rendered such essential services throughout the war,"[3] and that whether continued peace left him to rest upon his laurels, or new wars offered new opportunities, his reputation was for the time secure. Everywhere he went he was known, stared at, and sought after, for every news agency for five years had rung with his exploits; everywhere he was introduced and referred to as "the famous Major Rogers."

His first concern upon being placed at liberty from the restrictions of daily duty was to clear up certain troubling financial affairs. The preceding year[4] he had sent a memorial to the General Court of Massachusetts, asking £850 arrears of pay for his own and his company's service during the winter of 1755-56 at Fort William-Henry. This pay, already a source of vexatious and expensive lawsuits to him, had been heretofore refused on account of some doubt as to whether he was then in the service of the crown, or of Governor Shirley, or Governor Wentworth; and his memorial had been referred to the New Hampshire Assembly for a decision. Immediately, therefore, he proceeded to Portsmouth, to urge his claim before the provincial assembly. On June 5 the legislature read his memorial, and on June 27, the last day of us session, Rogers, equipped with recommendations from Johnson and Amherst,[5] and his muster-rolls, was admitted to speak in his own favour.

When he finished speaking it was after noon; the legislators were tired and hungry, and could think of nothing but that the hour at which they were to be prorogued had struck; and as he had omitted to bring with him his vouchers, the only adequate evidence of his rights, he was called into the chamber and told

3. *Dartmouth Mss.*, Rogers to the King, March 13, 1775.
4. March 9th, 1760.
5. *Johnson Mss.*, 24, 84.

that no action could then be taken.[6] Not until the beginning of 1763, two years later, when he was again free to appear in person before the house, did he receive a part payment of two hundred and thirty-five pounds.[7]

Meanwhile, during this spring and summer, a more important and more interestingly personal matter was engrossing his attention. When he had returned to his native colony after an absence of six years, he had at once taken steps to renew his acquaintance, under his now advantageous circumstances, with the best families of the province. He was received with especial favour in Portsmouth, where the constant reception of official reports of his deeds during the war had made him a figure of very real prominence; and was undoubtedly given an entry into circles which, in even that democratic town, would before have disdained him. Among the friendships which he formed was one with the family of the Reverend Arthur Browne, the most respected and best obeyed clergyman in the capital, then a white haired but still sternly erect and commanding figure of sixty-two, entering upon his twenty-sixth year of service as rector of Queen's Chapel.[8] He was the son of a Scotch veteran of the battle of the Boyne, and, having grown up in Drogheda and Dublin in Ireland, had received his degree from Trinity College, in the latter city, in 1729. Only a year previously Dean Berkeley had embarked for the Bermudas on his philanthropic project of establishing a circle of Protestant missions to convert the savage western world. This half-philosophic, half-evangelical scheme or the great prelate's had instilled a missionary fire into the brain of the young man; and immediately upon his ordination he crossed the seas to take charge of King's Chapel in Providence, Rhode Island, whence he was called in six years to Portsmouth. He was broadly educated, though of a conservative temper, and, despite a reputation for austerity and even harshness of mind, especially

---

6. *New Hampshire Province Papers,* VI, 790-794.
7. *Idem,* VI, 866.
8. For this biographical information see W. B. Sprague, *Annals of the American Pulpit,* New York, 1857-69,V, 76; C. R. Batchelder, *History of the Eastern Diocese,* Claremont, N. H., 1876,Vol. I, p. 165 ff.

towards his family of nine children, had become one of the most influential men in the community. He had published several tracts and sermons, notably one on *The Folly and Perjury of the Rebellion in Scotland* (1746).

In the Browne home, Rogers met and fell in love with the youngest daughter, Elizabeth, a beautiful girl of nineteen, and into this domestic circle he determined to push himself. Apart from all reasons of sentiment, he could have taken no step more advantageous. He had no fixed abode, and marriage would give him an opportunity to establish himself permanently at Portsmouth, in a position sociably enviable, and commanding distinct commercial privileges in the career of real-estate speculation to which, in the event of continued peace, he was then looking forward.

On the other hand, the honour bestowed upon the Browne household by the proposals of the dashing Major was an indubitable one. It seems hard to record that although the chief person concerned, Elizabeth herself, was not in entire harmony with the arrangement, plans for the union went on apace. As to her attitude, we have her own words in a statement which the unfortunate progress of events wrung from her many years after, at a time when her life must have seemed to her nearly wrecked by this marriage contracted at so tender an age:

> When I entered into matrimony, in June, 1761, with Col. Robert Rogers, he was a person of character and. distinction; though I married him solely in obedience to the will of my parents and friends.[9]

How real was this pressure—how much the union was against her will, and how much, in the light of her later injuries, she may have forgotten an original prepossession in the bridegrooms favour—it is impossible to say; but the whole spirit of household government then, and the temper of her father, were such that feeble protestations of her own would not have availed much.

---

9. Petition of Elizabeth Rogers to the General Assembly of New Hampshire, February 11th, 1778. No separate account is given in these pages of the divorce suit of Rogers' wife, but the grounds upon which it was based and granted will appear in detailed statements in the course of the narrative.

On June 30, 1761, the day on which the bride celebrated her twentieth birthday, she was led to the altar in Queen's Chapel by the tall and soldierly commander; and her own father, in the church over which he presided and where she had worshipped since her childhood, read the service which united them.[10] They returned after the ceremony to the home of the Brownes, for Rogers had as yet made no provision for a separate establishment. The honeymoon was brief. Six days after the wedding, there came to the major, from New York, the summons to a new campaign; and the husband caught up his arms, said a hasty farewell to his new and intimate connections, and was off to a farther frontier than any he had yet served upon.[11]

This frontier was the great undefined borderland between the Carolinas and the lands of the Cherokee Indians. The struggle now going on there was a reverberating echo of the far greater struggle that had just been fought out along the Ohio and the St. Lawrence—a dying glow of the heat of the conflict that had run from the north-eastern tip of the crescent which bounded the American colonies to its south-western extremity. In the decades previous to the Seven Years War the Cherokees were the natural allies of the English; but early in the conflict the French had begun to tamper with them and estrange them.[12]

In this they were aided by the blundering and bullying policy of the royal governor himself, one Lyttleton, who loaded the In-

10. Records of the Queen's Chapel, Portsmouth, New Hampshire.
11. Petition of Elizabeth Rogers to the General Assembly of New Hampshire, February 11th, 1778.
12. Edward McCready, *South Carolina under the Royal Government*, New York, 1899, pp. 330-350; W. Roy Smith, *South Carolina as a Royal Province*, New York, 1903, pp. 186, 208—225. "When the war with the Cherokees began, the Assembly resolved, in | February, 1760, to provide for seven troops of rangers of seventy-five men each, to be continued in the pay of the province until July 1st. ...An eighth troop was added in January, 1761, forming a regiment of six hundred men. Continued in service until October 1st, 1761, they took part in the Indian campaigns of Colonels Montgomery and Grant. The number of troops was reduced to four on October 1st, 1761, to two on April 1st, 1762, and the remainder were disbanded, July 1st, 1762." (Smith, p. 186.)

dians with indignities when they should have been treated with diplomatic kindness, and finally marched into their country to force an unwelcome treaty down their throats. Upon his return homeward the infuriated nation rushed down upon the innocent and defenceless families of the frontier in such force that a hurried call was sent northward for help. On April 1st, 1760, 1200 men under Colonel Montgomery, despatched by Amherst from the armies set free by the surrender of Quebec and Montreal, reached Charleston; and they, together with seven companies of partisan fighters raised by the governor, sufficed to defend the border during the summer. In February, 1761, a few days before Rogers arrived in New York from the west, Lieutenant Colonel James Grant, with whom the ranger had been associated at Fort Edward two years before, received orders to embark for the relief of the province. This expedition of Grant's, remarkable as the school in which a half-dozen such Revolutionary officers as Moultrie, Pickens, Laurens, and Marion learned their first lessons in war, invaded the territory in May, 2600 strong; and a month later, marching up the beautiful valley of the Salida, his army attacked and completely defeated the savages. A fortnight more of burning and pillaging reduced the farms of the tribes to desolate wastes; and returning early in August to Fort Prince Henry, he received the now submissive chief of the Cherokees, and transmitted him to Charleston to sue for peace.

So matters stood when, on August 20th, 1761, Rogers arrived at the capital of South Carolina, having come boldly overland in a full month's journey through Virginia and North Carolina with Colonel Byrd and a few Indian guides.[13] His advent had been long expected. Certain members of his old corps had been fighting under Grant since early spring; and as early as November of the preceding year, he himself had been mentioned as billeted for a command at Fort Loudon.[14] Three days after his arrival he set out northward, and travelling the one hundred and fifty miles to the border of the Cherokee country, assumed at Fort Prince George the command of an

13. *South Carolina Gazette*, June 6th, 1761; August 22nd, 1761.
14. *Idem*, September 13th, November 22nd, 1760; February 7th, May 30th, 1761.

independent company. His new post was worth £560 a year, and represented a fulfilment of Amherst's promise of a "substantial reward to follow his services."[15]

Rogers was too late for the active service of real warfare, but under Grant's orders he was engaged in scouting the country, even to the foot of the rugged, pine-grown hills that stretched their great flanks away toward the smoky summits of the Blue Ridge, and in helping hold in awe the great extent of plain and valley recently subjugated.[16]

In a later account he described. the fascination for him of the wide savannahs of grass, alternating with spacious forests of magnolia, tulip, gum, and oak, and breaking, to the west, into the misty mountainous country, where the limitless expanse of upland, embrowning under the August sun, rounded into vast knobs across whose hazy outline distant clouds of birds united like a slender wisp of smoke; and he touched also upon the discomforts of the sultry, thunderous weather, and the pestiferous clouds of mosquitoes.

In September he was withdrawn to the post called Ninety-six, for peace once more reigned on the border;[17] and here, half-way between the upper branches of the Sabine and the Savannah, in a country still hilly and full of an interesting Indian life, he lingered until the departure of nearly every other portion of Grant's force in December. Early in spring, while still retaining command of his now idle company, he was empowered by the provincial governor to raise volunteers up-colony, for a new regiment demanded for northern service by Amherst. In this he achieved remarkable success, beating up, from the towns north of Charleston, more than one hundred men within two months.[18] He was not interested in mere recruiting, however, and chafed to be permitted to return to the north.

---

15. *P. R. O., C. O. 5*, Volume 154, number 18; Rogers to Hillsborough, November 17th, 1771.

16. *South Carolina Gazette,* August 22nd, 1761.

17. *Idem,* November 1st, 1761.

18. *Idem,* December 19th, 1761; April 10th and June 5th, 1762. In May, it may be noted, a privateer was fitted out in Charleston harbour for use against the Spaniards by Rogers' brother James, and christened *Major Rogers.*

Finally, on August 1st, he completed his enlistments, sending forty men into Charleston in one day; and on October 9th, together with Lieutenant Ramsay, Amherst's special enlisting agent, he sailed for New York in the brig *Hannah*.[19] The command of his company he had given up on the first of July, when it was finally disbanded. In his whole employment in the south, he had undergone no very exciting experience, and had been given no opportunity to prove himself more than an efficient garrison officer; but he had greatly enlarged his acquaintance with the American colonies, and with the Indians of the west.

Early in November, after a brief stay in New York, Rogers was received with cordiality at his home in Portsmouth, from which he had been absent nearly a year and a half.[20] In January of 1763, as has been noted, he again presented to the Assembly his claim for deferred pay during 1755, and had it in part allowed; and at the same time new personal difficulties forced him to shape more carefully his business affairs, while he began to resume that interest in New Hampshire and New York lands which his summons to South Carolina had interrupted. Even before beginning his services in the Seven Years' War he had been involved in several minor actions for debt, now as defendant, now as plaintiff, and had signed one bond of £130 to a neighbour at Merrimac named William Allds. Although his present liabilities rendered his financial situation precarious, he now plunged into a series of land litigations with Allds, who claimed a prior right to Rogers farm at Merrimac, and lost them all, with heavy costs.[21] Another venture was similarly fruitless.

A year before, following a proclamation by Governor Colden of New York that the close of the war had opened for settlement the uncleared country above the Mohawk, Rogers and several fellow officers had petitioned for a grant of 25,000 acres on the shores of Lake George. but had been thwarted by the protests of the Mohawks Indians, conjoined with a stop-

---

19. South Carolina Gazette , August 6th, October 2nd, and October 16th, 1762.
20. Elizabeth Rogers Petition to the General Assembly of New Hampshire, February 11th, 1778.
21. *Idem.*

page by the crown of all such grants. Now, ably seconded by his associates, he renewed his claim, but without success.[22] His only prudential business measure was the purchase of a share of a Suncook sawmill.

He spent much of his time between Portsmouth and Rumford, and his improvidence, and a tendency toward dissipation, troubled and angered his father-in-law. On December 20th, 1762, by the expedient of loaning him £1000, the minister forced him to part with his 500 acres of land at Rumford, with three negro slaves, and "one Indian Boy named Billy, aged thirteen," which Browne at once transferred to a brother to hold in trust for Elizabeth Rogers.

During the spring the good pastor seems finally to have lost patience with his son-in-law. In April he made out a bill for the board and lodging of the major and his family, amounting, together with small sums paid his washerwoman, shoemaker, and tailor, to £2600; and adding to it the £1000 paid for his farm, and £500 for personal property given him, secured a writ and set a sheriff upon his heels. All his available property—it was but £50—was attached, and he was forced to give bond for the payment of the remainder of the debt.[23] His wife still remained, in a sense, loyal to him, but he was more and more estranged from her family.

During the worried months that followed his return from the Carolinas, Rogers retained his majority and was an intent observer of public affairs, in momentary readiness to resume his active command under Amherst's orders. His consistent hope was to win promotion in the colonial service; and, as he found ground for doubting that military affairs would present him many more opportunities, he temporarily fixed his ambitions upon appointment to a civil post, preferably the command of a western garrison. To this end he asked permission to go to England, as had several of his brother provincials, to urge before the home government the claim his services gave

22. Johnson mss., 24, 104.
23. These accounts, bills, and writs are still preserved at the Secretary of State's office at Concord, New Hampshire.

him upon a higher office; Johnson, however, partly because he wished to keep the experienced ranger at hand for frontier service, more largely because a growing distrust of Rogers' character made him feel that it would be dangerous to put the ranger in the way of responsible promotion, steadfastly refused to permit his departure.[24]

If the major chafed, it was not for long. In April he began to hear murmurs of widespread discontent throughout the savage nations of the west. Toward the end of the month these grew stronger, until news reached him in New Hampshire that the commandant of Detroit, alarmed at the congregation near that post of a great host of the Algonquin races, had sent an appeal for reinforcements to headquarters. The Indians along the Susquehanna were in arms against the encroaching white settlers, and from widely scattered posts along the Ohio and the Great Lakes came rumours of impending trouble. Fort Miami on March 30th reported the uprising of the Shawnee, and continued despatches from about Detroit reflected the increasing uneasiness of the savages there. The French had had no right, the tribes were complaining, to cede the red man's country to the English; and the irresistible trenching of the sturdy frontier farmer upon their hunting grounds beyond the Alleghanies filled them with resentful dismay. Finally, on May 10th, Amherst, sceptical and impatient as he was of the attitude of the Indians, announced that he would summon a meeting of the chiefs to have the terms of the treaty of peace explained to them, and began making preparations for the employment, if necessary, of harsher measures. A few days earlier Rogers had received an appointment as captain of one of the New York independent companies, in the room of a resigned officer, and had started west to Albany.[25]

Events now daily opened before him the new arena of action. As during the month all the border country of New York, Pennsylvania, and Virginia began to feel the still half-veiled fury of the western confederacy, the widespread nature and serious import of the uprising first began to be understood; though not

24. *Dartmouth Mss.*, Rogers to Dartmouth, March 13, 1775. *Johnson Mss.*, 12, 22.
25. *South Carolina Gazette,* May 14th, 1763.

until June 4th, 1763, when definite news of the insurrection reached New York from Fort Pitt and Detroit, was it evident that by a concerted plan the whole north-west was expressing its hatred of British aggression. Within ten days Amherst, who believed on June 1st that the whole affair would end in scattering and isolated outbreaks, and that even the minor posts were in no danger, had recognized his error, and determined to raise three full regiments and to equip smaller expeditions of relief.[26]

Reinforcements to the number of one hundred men had set out for Detroit, nearly a month before, with provisions and arms, and more were at once made ready. On June 16th Captain Dalyell, Amherst's aid, brought news from Albany that the first force had been attacked by night as it rested twenty-four miles from its goal, and driven back toward Niagara with the loss of forty men and all their stores.[27] Preparations for the march of a larger relief party were at once, and with redoubled energy, set on foot, and the honour of heading it allotted to Dalyell. Rogers was now at New York, and received with some chagrin the news of Dalyell's appointment to a command for which he felt himself the obvious candidate. Nevertheless, as he boasted later:[28]

It was with alacrity that I put myself forward under an inferior officer, nominated to an artificial rank for the oc- casion, it being matter of indifference to whom the credit of a dangerous enterprise was entrusted, so that he was signalized in a prompt obedience to his country.

While he hurriedly gathered together the members of the slender company over which he had just assumed command, and posted northward through Albany to Lake Erie, his superior collected two hundred men from the 55th and the 80th regiments of regulars, just arrived from the siege of Havana, and as hastily followed him. At Niagara they halted long enough to secure boats, and to equip them with ammunition, fresh provisions, and small cannon. While they tarried, there came the news

26. *Bouquet Papers*, 44, B21, 634, pp. 262-270.
27. *Documents Relative to the Colonial History of New York*, VII, 534.
28. P. R. O., C. O. 5, Volume 154, number 18.

of the treacherous massacre of the garrison at Venango, of the loss, rumoured or assured, of Sandusky, Miami, Mackinac, and Presqu' Isle, and of the redoubling of the attacks on Detroit.

It was plain that the western woods were all aflame, and that scores of Indian villages and tribes were in arms. At the same time the busied soldiers heard full accounts of the organization of the war by Pontiac, chief of the Ottawa, and learned something of the resources and numbers of the great Indian army under his command, then concentrated about Detroit, against which their little column was to pit its strength.[29]

Rogers first meeting with Pontiac had been three years before, during the course of the memorable journey he had taken in the autumn and winter of 1760 to assume possession of the western forts surrendered by the French.[30] On the fourth of November of that year, he had set out westward from Presqu' Isle with seven barges, coasting along the southern shore of Lake Erie. The weather was rough, and an overcast sky and cold drizzling rain were accompanied by a wind which sent the waves breaking high over the prows of their boats; the shoreline, level and high-timbered, showed the once-blazing foliage of the Indian summer hanging dreary and dark in the chilling blast, or whirling in sodden clouds over the wet beach. By the seventh, having skirted the lake for nearly forty miles, they had reached the mouth of the Chogage River,[31] a considerable stream flowing down placidly through tall, free groves of oak, hickory, and locust, near the site of the present city of Cleveland.

Here, putting in for an hour's refreshment, they were hailed by a party of Indians wearing the paint and garb of Ottawas, who represented themselves as ambassadors of Pontiac, and in the name of "the king and lord of the country" commanded Rogers to await his presence. In the course of an hour the chief arrived; he

---

29. Francis Parkman, *Conspiracy of Pontiac*, Boston, 1851; *Diary of the Siege of Detroit,* edited by Franklin B. Hough, Albany, 1860; H. M. Utley, *History of Michigan*, New York, 1906, I, 243-291; Silas Farmer, *History of Detroit,* Detroit, 1809, I, 231-241.
30. Rogers, *Journals*; Rogers *Concise Account of North America*, p. 240.
31. So called by Rogers. Variously conjectured to have been the Chagrin, the Cuyahoga, and the Grand. See T. M. Cooley's *Michigan*, Boston, 1885, p. 42.

advanced and "with an air of majesty and princely grandeur," and according to the respectful major a grave salutation, demanded of him how he dared enter unannounced the Indian country. Rogers quietly informed him of his mission to Detroit, diplomatically adding that the expulsion of the French could not fail to benefit the savages in increased privileges in hunting and trade.

In brief rejoinder Pontiac held out a small string of *wampum*, in token that the rangers must not depart without his leave, and retired to deliberate in council upon the matter. Although the *calumet* of peace was smoked during the course of evening, Rogers posted double guards, and himself remained awake all night, until at daybreak the conference was continued. Amid puffs at the re-lighted pipe, and in measured syllables, the chief now declared that he was satisfied with the English officer's statement of his purposes in invading the country; that he wished to live in amity with his new neighbours; that he would warn all the Indian towns along the shore and about the mouth of the Detroit river to offer no obstacle to the British advance; and that he would supply the company with parched corn and meat, and detail one hundred warriors to help them transport their provisions.[32]

Continued rainstorms confined the soldiers to camp for several days, during which time the savages held a veritable carnival in marketing their wild turkeys and venison. Meanwhile Pontiac had withdrawn. On November 29th, when Rogers' lieutenants, in presence of a vastly larger French force, cut loose the white lilies of the Bourbons from the flagstaff at Detroit, and raised in their stead the colours of England, seven hundred Indians, standing by with their chief, lifted a mighty cry of wonderment and acclamation. They had been ready but a few days before to fall in annihilating strength upon the English, but had been restrained by Pontiac.

---

32. "In 1763, when I went to throw provisions into the garrison at Detroit, I sent this Indian a bottle of brandy by a Frenchman. His councillors advised him not to eat it, insinuating that it was poisoned, and sent with a design to kill him; but Ponteach, with a nobleness of mind, laughed at their suspicions, saying it was not in my power to kill him, who had so lately saved his life." *Concise Account*, p. 244.

During Rogers' stay at Detroit, he often saw the proud chieftain, who dwelt with his squaws and retainers on Pèche Isle, a high, wooded islet nearby in Lake St. Clair, and—always with strong deference to Pontiac's intense personal pride and egotism—engaged him in repeated interviews. He learned much concerning the western country, and the empire which even then the lake Indians had formed, and discovered in him "great strength of judgment, great thirst after knowledge, and great jealousy of his own respect and honour." The chief offered the major a part of his kingdom if he would take him overseas to England and initiate him into British military, social, and commercial affairs; but at the same time made it clear that he would expect to be treated abroad with the courtesy due an independent and equal potentate. He was decisive in his assertions that the country of the western tribes was not to be bartered about among European nations as a piece of conquered territory.

Now Rogers was guiding a party over this same route, but in arms against the chief, and amid widespread signs of his hostile power. On the seventh of July, in calm bright weather, the force set out, and, soon leaving the thunder and mist of the falls far behind, were by nightfall well out along the full expanse of the lake. They numbered nearly two hundred, in part veterans who had fought battles under the British flag in many climes, in part experienced provincial scouts; Rogers had direct command of the twenty men most experienced in wood service, and guided the expedition as it proceeded. Dalyell, who had served continuously in America since 1756, was of indubitable bravery and experience, there seems early to have been some jealous friction between the two men.

Through successive days of oppressive heat they coasted the south shore, moving as fast as they might; the lake was calm, the heavy green tops of the fringing woods hung languidly motionless in the full effulgence of the sun, and the sky met the water at the horizon like an inverted mirror. They finally reached the charred, wrecked ruins of the fort at Presqu' Isle, the ground about it furrowed and littered with the works thrown up by the attacking savages; and a few days later Sandusky, where dusty trenches, converging upon a mound of ashes, and some half-burned timbers, told the same story of violence. At this point they landed to wreak vengeance upon a neighbouring village of the Wyandotte, and, after ravaging their cornfields, pushed on again by water for the mouth of the Detroit River.

When they arrived here on the evening of July 28th, all was still, for the savage host, lying only a few miles above, had not even a scout out to sound the alarm. Under cover of night, paddling as rapidly as possible, they ascended the stream, and in the misty dawn, making a final dash for the beleaguered fort, gained the protection of its guns just at sunrise. As they entered, the Indian besiegers broke the silence of a fortnight with a hot fusillade, and inflicted a trifling loss upon the hindmost boats; but nothing could stop the cheers of the garrison, worn as they were with constant watching, and as the soldiery disembarked, the streets of the French village rang with their rejoicing. The barracks could not accommodate the new arrivals, and they were quartered in the homes of the *habitants*.

The Indian army under Pontiac, then numbering more than two thousand warriors, had but recently withdrawn its main camp to a river marsh two miles above the post, whence it kept the town and fort constantly surrounded. Dalyell feared its withdrawal, and proposed an immediate attack, which was actually set on foot soon after midnight on the second day after his coming. By some it is said that a dispute between the provincials and the English regulars as to their relative fighting effectiveness was the mainspring behind the ill-judged advance. The commander's plans were betrayed to the Indians by the French about the post, and when in the heavy gloom just before the dawn of July 31st his little corps moved out from town along a road parallel to the river, and into the pitchy forest beyond, he was attacked in force.

The battle which followed is known as Bloody Run, for it surged and varied along the shores of a little stream which for hours ran crimson. The English column, stumbling along the darkness of the village road, with its flank protected by two can-non-bearing *bateaux* on the river opposite, was on the point of crossing this creek, when it was met in the face by the fire of the entrenched savages, forced back in confusion, re-attacked on the open side, and finally, as it still rallied stubbornly, pushed back among the first scattering houses of the town. Half of the offic-ers were killed in the first moments of the combat, and, despite the heroic efforts of the rearguard to keep open the communi-cations with the fort in the rear, the full body occupied several hours in its fighting retreat, which the Indians endeavoured re-peatedly to cut off. After their first fire the savages scattered, and from behind trees, wood piles, barns, and outbuildings poured a galling fusillade into the ranks of the troops, still bewildered in the slowly-dissipating darkness.

Rogers and his men early occupied a house beside the high-way, first expelling a troop of Indians, and from it covered their comrades retreat, until in a few moments they were themselves completely isolated. Many years later an eyewitness gave Park-man an account of the fighting from this building.[33]

The major entered with some of his own men, while many panic-stricken regulars broke in after him, in their anxiety to gain a temporary shelter. The house was a large and strong one, and the women of the neighbour-hood had crowded into the cellar for refuge. While some of the soldiers looked in blind terror for a place of con-cealment, others seized upon a keg of whiskey in one of the rooms, and quaffed the liquor with eager thirst, while others piled packs of furs, furniture, anything in reach, against the windows as a barricade. Panting and breathless, their faces moist with sweat and blackened with gunpowder, they thrust their muskets through the openings, and fired out upon the whooping assailants. At intervals a bullet sharply whizzed through a crev-ice, striking down a man, or rapping harmlessly against the partitions. The gray-haired master of the house, old

33. Francis Parkman, *The Conspiracy of Pontiac,* Boston, 1851, p. 475.

Campau, stood on a trap door to prevent the frightened soldiers seeking shelter among the women in the cellar. The screams of the half-stifled women below, the quavering war-whoops without, the shouts and curses of the soldiers, the groans of the wounded, mingled in a scene of clamorous confusion.

From their perilous position here Rogers and his men were saved by the hasty movement of the *bateaux*, which were rowed down to a position where the swivel cannon swept the woods and gardens about, and drove the savages away from their path in momentary disorder. Yet not a moment too soon the rangers fell upon the retreating main body, for as they parted by one door the foremost Indians leaped in at another.

At eight o'clock the troops, exhausted, crestfallen, and discouraged, re-entered the palisades they had so lately quitted. The night's sally had cost them dear, for they had lost their commander and sixty men. Dalyell had been killed in an act of impulsive bravery, running back, to save a comrade, and a Captain Grant had taken his place in the chief command. The Indians were greatly elated; their yells of triumph filled the woods, and swift runners were at once sent out to bear the joyful news far and wide. Nevertheless the English kept up a good heart. They had succeeded in inflicting some small injury upon the enemy, and they knew that their position, since the reinforcement of the garrison, was entirely safe.

For some months the siege dragged wearily and uneventfully on. When on August 13th a schooner and sloop were sent to Niagara for troops and supplies, Rogers took the opportunity to transmit to Johnson a partial journal of the siege, extending from its beginning until July 4th, material for which he had obtained from the officers of the fort;[34] and in October he inquired whether he would be relieved from garrison duty during the fall, and requested that his wife be given the same information.[35] On the twelfth of this month one of the chiefs represented to

---

34. In *Journals of the Siege of Detroit* published by Leonaur..
35. See the same volume, page 175.

Major Gladwin that the young braves were urgent to begin the winter hunts, and arranged a truce which permitted the soldiers to lay in a further store of provisions; none too soon, for they were subsisting on five pounds of flour and one half-gallon of wheat each week. At about the same time Pontiac wrote that his Indian followers had buried the hatchet, and "all the bad things had passed should be forgotten on both sides."

A few days later the smoke ceased to rise from their whilom encampment. Taking their women and children, the savages had departed southward. Peace had not been made, and the war—which, indeed, did not end for nearly a year—was only broken; but Detroit had little to fear until spring.[36]

In November Gladwin determined to reduce his garrison for the winter, and sent all but two hundred men east to Niagara, where they arrived near the end of the month. Rogers, accompanied by two Mohawk Indians, followed a few days later, relieved by a return to the security of the east.[37] Ever since the departure of the Indians the days had passed monotonously at Detroit, for it was unsafe to wander far from the fort, or to pursue stray game into the woods; the treachery of the French in the town nearby was constantly feared; the men, in a garrison so small, had to perform irksomely constant garrison duty; and their rations were limited in variety, as well as in quantity. For some time, apparently, the major lingered near in Niagara, partly on military duty, partly engaged in affairs of his own—affairs, too, of no very creditable nature. Of any specific misdeeds we know nothing, but it seems clear that he was concerned in the trade with the friendly tribes of the Mohawks and Delawares in the region, and was using his uniform, his commission, and his reputation in furthering his business ventures; while at the same time he was none too honest in his various dealings with associates in the Indian trade, and permitted one such trader, William McCracken, to forfeit a bond in his name. In the last years of the French war, and in the period since, except for the time he was engaged

36. *Bouquet Papers*, Canadian Archives, 1889, pp. 242 ff.
37. *Johnson Mss.*, 24, 22.

in the Carolina campaigns, he had been suspected of an illegal participation in the very traffic with the border tribes which it was his military duty to help regulate; and his open concern with it now brought him under the direct displeasure of Sir William Johnson at Johnson Hill.

Early in January, 1764, he surrendered his commission, and posted to New York; and on the twenty-second of that month, according to a rather cryptic letter of the period, he "escaped" to "precious" Connecticut by sea.[38] The exact nature and extent of his derelictions in Indian commerce are dubious, but they had sufficed to make for him powerful enemies.

On February 24th, Rogers was again at Rumford, looking after the farm which he had given over a year before to his father-in-law, and which was now held in his wife's name. He dined on this date with the Rev. Mr. Walker, and seems to have been hereabouts on brief errands of business repeatedly through the summer. Most of the year, however, he spent near or in Portsmouth, engrossed in his dealings in land. A number of the score or more of conveyances to which he was a party between his marriage and 1765 are dated during these months, and in all of them he signs himself as "of Portsmouth" or "now residing in Portsmouth." His absences from his wife's home, however, were frequent and lengthy, and she complains repeatedly that he scarcely succeeded, in all, in spending more than a few days with her. Nothing, indeed, is more significant of Rogers' real character than his consistent attitude toward the woman whom, as she herself reminded him,[39] he was "bound by the tenderest, most sacred ties to protect, succour, and comfort,"—his habitual neglect of her, the calm indifference with which he forgot for months at a time his entire connection with her, his failure to make any real provision for her separate maintenance.

Whatever may have been his object in marrying, it was plainly not to found a home. The excuse which his military services gave him for his neglect was far from valid now, when—no matter what his ambitions—his only immediate abstraction was with

38. *Johnson Mss.*, 8, 121 (McCracken to Johnson), and 12, 22 (Johnson to Gen. Gage).
39. Elizabeth Rogers petition.

his real-estate ventures. And although he was associated much with his brother, James Rogers, who had secured the grant of a tract of nearly twenty thousand acres lying east of Lake Champlain, in Vermont, he was seldom far from the capital; indeed, his most important project, culminating July 4th in the acquisition of three thousand acres at Readsboro, Vermont, he carried through without leaving the city, for the colony granted him the land in his capacity as a half-pay officer.[40] This property he was compelled immediately to mortgage to one Gysbert Fonda of Albany for £5600, while his wife's land he also placed under an encumbrance of £350. He was evidently deep in debt.[41]

In early March, 1765, Rogers—giving out that he was off for the West Indies—departed for England, upon the trip which in his own worldly interests he had so long meditated. His knowledge of the pronounced disapproval with which, in all capacities except the rather narrow one of Indian fighter, Johnson and his American associates viewed him, made it seem imperative that he seek his coveted promotion on the other side of the water. Colonel Gladwin, with whom he had been associated at Detroit, was gone in October, tired of the American service, yet certain that he had fulfilled his duty; he was presented to the sovereign, and complimented upon his achievements.[42] Some such distinction Rogers hoped to receive, while he wished above all to secure an administrative appointment in the king's employ, whether in Europe, India, or America.

For some time past he had seen junior officers elevated above him merely because they had found time to present themselves at London, and opportunity to secure the influence of court friends. One Gorham, for example, a mere captain of rangers who had served for two years under his command, was now established as a lieutenant-colonel over his head.[43] He was, moreover, anxious to see the land of his fathers; anxious to leave the

40. *New Hampshire Province Papers,* VII, I; *New Hampshire Province and State Papers,* X, 207.
41. In later years the farm of Rogers at Concord, with the old Rogers house, was occupied by his wife, then divorced. The house stood for many years, marking the virtual outskirts of Concord to travellers coming down the river. Lyford's *Concord,* I, 619.
42. *Documents Relative to the Colonial History of New York,* VII, 666.
43. *Dartmouth Mss.,* March 13, 1775.

complaints of his wife, and the importunities of his creditors; anxious to investigate the glamour of metropolitan existence; and anxious to publish two books upon which he had meditated during his leisure moments. In the English book marts of the hour there was a ready demand for military accounts of the glorious struggle just closed, and for geographical descriptions of the vast realms just added to the crown.

His chief activities in London, therefore, were political and literary. His exploits had well advertised him, and his advent attracted general notice. Old military friends crowded about him, and with the recommendations to various gentlemen of prominence which he had brought with him, he shortly became known among the lesser notables of the season. In the magazines of the time[44] is found frequent mention of his career and his person, and upon the streets his tall, sturdy figure, carried with an easy boldness of demeanour, was frequently pointed out. He resorted to the parties and clubs at which officers, retired and active, were found, and won speedily a deserved reputation for joviality and good fellowship.

Tradition has still perpetuated stories of how, when accosted one lonely night by a highwayman on Hounslow Heath, he peremptorily knocked him down and dragged him away to justice; of how he appeared, on a wager, at a fashionable ball in the uncouth garb of a backwoods hunter; of how once, deep in his glasses with a merry company, he bet he could tell the greatest lie, and, relating the strange but true story of his father's death, was vociferously awarded the palm.[45] Indeed, he laid at this time the real foundation for a very considerable and lasting popularity in London—one which endured through all the compromising vicissitudes which later brought him an exiled petitioner to the capital.

Of his picturesque appearance at the time, and of some of

44. *Gentleman's Magazine,* November and December, 1760; December, 1765; March, 1766. *The Monthly Review,* XXIV, 9, 22, and 242. *The Critical Review,* 1766, p. 151; 1765, p. 386.
45. John Farmer and J. B. Moore, *Collections, Topographical, Historical, and Biographical, Relating Principally to New Hampshire,* Concord, 1822-4, Volume I, 240.

the grounds upon which his reputation was based, we may judge from a crudely designed and coloured print-portrait of him which ten years later was exposed for sale in all the shop-windows, with the legend beneath, "Major Rogers, the famous Ranger."[46] It was reproduced in Germany, and copies of it are even yet preserved. They show us a tall, heavy man, smooth-shaven, with a countenance pleasantly open and regular, but coarsely delineated. He is in full uniform, with long hair partially hidden by a regulation cockade; a heavy rifle is thrown over the hollow of his arm; a powder-horn is suspended from his shoulder by a band of Indian workmanship; an embroidered belt, fastened by a heavy silver buckle, encircles his waist; his lower limbs are encased in leggings, and a sword hangs by his side. This military and energetic bearing, however, heightened as it is by the relief with which his sinewy figure is outlined against a gloomy forest background, from whose shades indistinctly push two naked savages, is not borne out by his expression or features. The jaw is harsh, the lips full and heavy, the large nose and prominent eyes almost cold and phlegmatic in aspect; the glance and the set of the features, while direct enough, still seem calculating and evasive. While the face is clearly that of a man of action, largely wanting in lines of thought, it is far from being indicative of the rugged, daredevil energy with which we associate Rogers' name.

To further his designs for an American appointment Rogers soon set about the preparation and publication of his *Journals*, or the diary he had kept of his movements during the Seven Years War, and of another book which he called *A Concise Account of North America*. These appeared simultaneously in October, 1765, from the press of John Millan, a Whitehall stationer of some prominence, in small octavo dress, and sold for four and five shillings respectively. Both were at once favourably reviewed by the critical magazines, which took evident pleasure in introducing the military hero in his literary capacity. The *Monthly Review* said:

---

46. This print, first struck off on October 1st, 1776, is described in Smith's *British Mezzotint Portraits*. It was reprinted in *Geschichte der Kriege in und ausser Europa, Elfter Theil*, Nurnberg, 1777.

Few of our readers are unacquainted with the name, or ignorant of the exploits of Major Rogers, who with so much reputation headed the provincial corps called Rangers during the whole course of our late successful wars in America—a brave, active, judicious officer. To him we are obliged, in the *Concise Account*, for the most satisfactory description we have yet been favoured with of the interior parts of the immense continent which victory has so lately added to the British Empire.

Of the *Journals* it said:

The author, who has given undoubted proofs of his bravery and skill (wrote) like an honest, a sensible, and a modest man (and that his work was) authentic, important, and necessary to a thorough understanding of the late military operations in North America.

The other periodicals similarly joined praise of his literary achievements in the same articles. The reviewer for the *Critical Review* said:

The fatigues Major Rogers has undergone in the course of his duty would seem almost incredible were they not confirmed by the unquestionable relations of others.

The estimate of his merits as an author is more guarded, but "the prepossessing openness with which he writes" is praised, and portions of his work are spoken of as "valuable," and other parts as "new and curious."[47]

In truth, the two books were interesting and timely contributions to the British knowledge of current affairs. The *Journals* followed his field career, day by day, month by month, from the moment when as an obscure captain he arrived with his company of rangers below Crown Point till that in which he received the surrender of the outermost forts of the French. They display no sense of historical proportion, for several insignificant scouts receive as much space as the operations of Abercrombie

---

47. Monthly Review, January, 1766; Critical Review, November, 1765.

or Amherst against Montcalm; and they are written, as one of his critics noted, in a "dry unambitious" style. They are honest and accurate in tone, however, and, while intimately personal, seldom if ever give evidence of prejudice or jealousy in their outlook upon the affairs of fellow and superior officers. Their chief value lies in the facts which, despite Rogers' monotonous lack of emphasis, we may glean from his pages concerning the defeat of Abercrombie, the victories of Amherst and Haviland below Montreal, and the account of his own journey upon the Great Lakes; their chief interest lies in the fuller narrative of one or two of his most brilliant skirmishes, the unconscious colour that creeps between the lines which describe his various scouts, and the rather bitter recital of his dangers and hardships on the St. Francis raid. The style is awkward and poverty-stricken, and the ill-calculated space given at times to trivial letters and orders betrays hasty composition.

The *Concise Account,* which bears evidence of more careful literary workmanship, is a manual of information regarding the colonies of North America, their natural advantages, and the location and character of the colonial settlements and outposts. Large portions of it, especially the historical sketches of the provinces, are mere compilations from previous publications, but all the regions from Nova Scotia to the Carolinas, from New York to Detroit, which Rogers had traversed in person, are described in full, and—especially in the case of distinctly frontier phases of existence—with acute observation. A too-pervading formality unfortunately restrains the writer from ever falling into a genuinely racy, fresh vein. An appendix contains a popularly exaggerated description of various wild animals, and a considerable treatment of the manners, customs, and character of the Indians—the latter the cream of the book. A real sympathy, if some triteness, is brought by Rogers to this exposition of savage life. He recognizes the errors and weaknesses of the race, but he does ample honour to their virtues. In their domestic institutions he finds much that is admirable: their rigid if somewhat oblique ethics; the respect in which the aged are held; the fine appreciation of personal dignity which restrains the parent from chastising his child; their universal equanimity under the assaults of every passion (except revenge), "surpassing all but the most Christian philosophers;" their respectful unselfishness toward friends and allies.

What is far more distinctive in a rough, active frontiersman, Rogers expresses an almost town-bred admiration of the simple gentleness of their untutored minds, and the pastoral beauty and happiness of their roving life. In this respect he speaks most especially of the Illinois and Missouri, whose land he regarded as "the most salubrious and fertile in the world." He writes:

These people of any upon earth seem blessed in this world: here is health and joy, peace and plenty; care and anxiety, ambition and the love of gold, and every uneasy passion, seem banished from this happy region. The goodness of the country they inhabit renders their life enchantingly agreeable and easy.

And he presages with an apparent lingering of regret the coming day when the region must be occupied by a people whose studied refinement in "dress, equipage, and the modes of life" will shatter this existence of halcyon content; for he observed that the Indians insatiable fondness for spirituous liquors would clear the continent of them in a century.[48]

In short, Rogers attitude toward the savage race bespeaks a liberality almost anomalous in one whose earliest lesson was to fear and hate the redskin, and whose fame depended upon the success with which he had waged his campaigns against them and their Canadian leaders. This largeness of view expresses itself, again, in a sentiment which would now be called imperial patriotism. He regards the new domains as amongst the most fruitful and desirable upon earth, and rejoices everywhere that they have been given to the English race to be subdued and cultivated. Again and again he repeats, in effect, the declaration which follows the account in his *Journals* of the surrender of Montreal—that the wealth of the, Incas and Aztecs was as

---

48. *Concise Account of North America.*

nothing to that of the northern continent, and that the Anglo-Saxon peoples could not fail to find in it a home of wonderful scope and resource. The style of the second book, moreover, is solid and clear, and it amasses an amount of information, drawn from observation and research, that is far from contemptible. Altogether, there is no point at which we are more likely to be surprised into real respect for the Ranger than in the reading of his two treatises. They not merely exhibit his singular success in self-education, but for one of his education and profession reflect every credit upon his natural powers and abilities.

Rogers himself had no illusions as to the main defects of his work; in the preface to his *Journals* he attempts to disarm the critics by his statement that the work was written—

> .... not with silence and leisure, but among deserts, rocks, and mountains, amidst the hurries, disorders, and noise of war, and under that depression of spirits which is the natural consequence of exhausting fatigue.

While in the preface to his *Concise Account* he asserts that it is not his ambition to shine as a learned. historian, but merely to relate—

> .... such simple facts as may be useful to his country until he might resign his plume to someone with greater life and ornament.

It was generally understood[49] that both books were to be continued, and in the *Concise Account* appeared an advertisement of a third volume to contain a history of the Cherokee war and the siege of Detroit, with many maps and plans. The demand for this addition, which Rogers planned to sell at one guinea by subscription was, however, so slender that he abandoned the project. A seemingly trivial circumstance determined the nature of his third and last publication. That part of the *Concise Account* which had most struck the fancy of several reviewers was the description, among the pages devoted to the Indians, of the chief Pontiac, widely famed even in

49. *Monthly Review,* 34, 10.

England for his recent rebellion. Rogers had drawn him with a taciturn dignity which fired the imagination of the writer for the *Critical Review,* and at the close of his paragraph the latter made a suggestion upon which the major hastily acted. "The picture exhibited of the emperor Pontiac," he said, "is novel and interesting, and would appear to advantage in the hands of a great dramatic genius."

In February, 1766, four months later, and some weeks after Rogers had returned homeward from England, the tragedy *Ponteach* appeared from the press of John Millan, under a timid anonymity, but with the universal knowledge that Rogers was the author. Like the other volumes, it was published in small octavo, and sold for two shillings and sixpence. It closed disastrously Rogers' brief career as an author, for the press united in condemnation of it. "One of the most absurd productions we have ever seen," was the verdict of the *Monthly Review.*

> It is a great pity that so brave and judicious an officer should thus run the hazard of exposing himself to ridicule by an unsuccessful attempt to enliven the poet's bays with the soldier's laurels. In turning bard and writing a tragedy Rogers makes just as good a figure as would a Grub-street rhymester at the head of our author's corps of North American rangers.

Even the *Critical Review,* which had suggested the topic, admitted it could bestow no encomiums upon Rogers as a poet, and pronounced the drama unprecedentedly insipid and flat. The *Gentleman's Magazine* alone gave the play more than a few lines, and it did so only to point out the flimsiness of its plot and the "disgusting familiarity" of its language.

The major was followed at this time by an agent or secretary, named Nathaniel Potter—an educated and rather clever, but disreputable Englishman whom he had engaged in New Hampshire before sailing for England, and who had presumably accompanied him. Potter said of himself later that since meeting Rogers in early 1765 he "had continued to be much connected with him and used by him in various ways," while Johnson stated in 1767 that he had been hired because Rogers was so illiterate as to require someone to do business for him.[50]

If he were actually with the major at this time, he may be partially deserving of credit for the *Concise Account* and *Ponteach,* which represent a greater literary facility than do the *Journals* or Rogers' ordinary letters and reports; although the content of both is by internal evidence largely Rogers'. He may also have assisted the Ranger in one of his most original steps toward political preferment—the proposal of August 12, 1765, for a search after the Northwest Passage. In the memorial embodying this project, as presented to the king, Rogers set forth his unusual qualifications for the quest—knowledge of the country, capacity for making discoveries, strength of constitution, and talent for conciliating the Indians—and his certainty that there was such a passage, gained from "his assiduous prosecution of every possible inquiry" and his employment, at private expense, of Indians to explore the distant rivers to the Pacific and Arctic. He prayed to be given two hundred men, with whom he would proceed across the headwaters of the Mississippi, and down the Oregon to Puget Sound, thence following northward the western shore of the continent; the expedition would consume in all £28762 and three years' time. Although in a pathetic note he represented himself ruined by expensive lawsuits, his petition was refused by the Privy Council.[51]

In obtaining an appointment, however, Rogers was more successful. He bore a letter of introduction to the Lord Mayor,[52] and by Amherst and others was well recommended to Hillsborough, president of the Board of Trade; while in October, 1765, one of the intimate friends he had made, William Fitzherbert, was installed a commissioner of trade and plantations.[53] On the twelfth of that month he received his coveted post.[54] One of the November reviews of his *Journals*

---

50. *Johnson Mss.* 15; 106, 154.
51. *Documents Relative to the Colonial History of New York,* VII, 988.
52. Memorial, Rogers to Hillsborough, December 21st 1768.
53. *Gentleman's Magazine,* October, 1765.
54. Memorial, Rogers to Hillsborough, October 26th, 1769.

congratulated him upon his advancement,[55] and the colonial gazettes soon repeated the news in the colonies.[56] In December he sailed for home; and on January 10th it was made known that by royal direction General Gage at New York had appointed him commander of the troops at Mackinac (Michilimackinac), almost the westernmost, and one of the most important, of the British garrisons.[57]

55. *Critical Review*, November, 1765.
56. *Johnson Mss.*, 12, 22.
57. Memorial, Rogers to Hillsborough, October 26, 1769.

CHAPTER 4

The Governorship at Mackinac

In America Johnson and his associates heard the news of Rogers' appointment with indignant apprehension. None of his superiors in the colonies considered him even remotely fitted for a position of executive trust, and there was a general conviction that with his incapacity for governmental affairs was allied a want of principle and character that might make him actively dangerous. The same officers that in 1755 had been loath to believe the charges of rascality brought against him as a counterfeiter and enlisting officer were now the first to express their amazement at his new promotion. Gage wrote to Johnson characterising him as morally untrustworthy, and the latter replied in the most emphatic terms.[1]

> It was I, who for his readiness first made him an officer, and had him continued in the service, where he soon became puffed up with pride and folly, from the extravagant encomiums and notices of the provinces. This spoiled a good ranger, for he was fit for nothing else; neither has nature calculated him for a large command in that service. He has neither understanding nor principles, as I could sufficiently show. The character you have given him is just, and I am astonished that the government should have thought of such an employment for him.

Several other letters of the Indian commissioner expressed the same disgust. The concurrence of the general public in his opin-

---

1. January 23, 1700. *Johnson Mss.* 12, 22.

ion, moreover, proves that it was no mere rankling prejudice, nor the effect of his enmity toward Amherst and the other men to whom Rogers probably owed his appointment. Indeed, in a letter of a slightly subsequent date Johnson alludes to the universal disapproval of Rogers, and expresses a charitable wish that, extricating himself from his debts, he may belie his reputation.

> He does not appear to be much esteemed, and it gives me pain to find a useful, active man struggling under the disadvantage of distress and a bad name; for he would have done much better if he had not been exalted too much by the people here, who now appear foremost in debasing him. I hope he will act a proper part at Mackinac, prove of service to the public, extricate himself from his difficulties, and deserve a better character than the public has for some time bestowed upon him. I wish the government had found a better or more adapted employment for him.[2]

But he makes it clear elsewhere that to him this was a highly improbable consummation. Johnson, indeed, was at this moment particularly jealous of the western administration, and wished no officers at the frontier posts upon whose integrity and ability he could not rely. During the whole preceding summer he had been engaged in making peace with the still unnamed nations under Pontiac, and had sent a command under Colonel George Croghan into the Illinois country to treat with them; and now he was busied with large plans for the preservation and development of the trade with the distant tribes. The French west of the Mississippi he believed to be creating among the Indians of the north-west an active opposition to the English occupation, and to English commerce. He wrote:

> Those of the Illinois are continually among the savages with immense cargoes of goods, instilling the most pernicious sentiments into the minds of a credulous people, and diverting the trade from its proper channels.[3]

2. To Major Moncrieffe Gage. *Johnson Mss.* 12, 27.
3. *Documents Relative to the Colonial History of New York*, VII, 775.

Croghan had persuaded the peoples along the Illinois, the Wabash, the Chicago, the St. Joseph, and the Saginaw and La Baye to petition for a large extension of British commercial facilities toward their villages, and Johnson was earnestly trying to persuade the Board of Trade of the urgent necessity, for both political and economic reasons, of granting this extension. He wrote:

> It is not in the power of my officer to permit traders to go from Detroit or Mackinac, and the Indians will be supplied this year chiefly from the Illinois, which is all French property. If trading posts are not established at proper places in that country, soon the French will carry the best part of the trade over the Mississippi, on whose left bank they are building a strong fort.[4]

He had for some time been pushing a plan the main provision of which was the establishment, at each western military post, of a commissary of Indian affairs, as responsible to him for the conduct of the trade and the maintenance of amicable relations with the savages as the commandant was to Gage in military matters. In particular, now, he was urging the establishment of such commissaries at Detroit, Mackinac, and Fort Chartres on the Mississippi, the three stations which dominated the western country.[5] That these local superintendents should do their work well it was essential that the regular governors at their respective forts should willingly and honestly cooperate with them. The plan, moreover, was not yet a certainty, and until it was put in operation the governors would administer Indian affairs, still delicate and sensitive as these were. When, therefore, Rogers widely known for his unscrupulousness, and already covertly defiant of Johnson—was given the chief authority at Mackinac, the latter had reason to be sincerely alarmed.

Rogers appeared before the northern superintendent at Johnson Hall early in February, sending his *Journals* on in advance "for perusal;" and it was clear that he would soon be at his post. At once Johnson arrived at a determination that the major

---

4. *Idem.*, p. 788.
5. *Idem.*, p. 808.

must be so hampered in his new office by restrictions, so bound by instructions, and so watched by his superiors, that all the gates to possible wrongdoing would be barred, and no latitude left to him to obstruct more than passively the plans of the Indian department or of Gage. He said in a letter to the general:[6]

I am of opinion that he should be tied up in such a manner as shall best prevent him doing mischief. . . . If he is bound by my orders in everything relating to Indian affairs, and obliged to transmit regular reports of all transactions, I think he will not have it in his power to do as much harm as otherwise; though to prevent him from doing any is impossible, for he has been concerned in trade, and will again be, with those of his connections in that quarter. By his being commandant he will have it in his power to confine the trade in great measure to himself and friends; neither would he stick at saying anything to the Indians, to effect any of his purposes. . . . The only thing to be done is to point out from whom he is to take his orders respecting Indian affairs, and the channels through which his reports are to be transmitted; and to limit his expenses to pipes, tobacco, and a little liquor—unless when he may be ordered to meet any body of Indians; and whenever they shall address him to send a faithful copy of his speeches.

His recommendations were followed. It was clearly Johnson's haunting fear that the pressure of Rogers' obligations would force him to take criminal means to supply his wants, and it was to this end that the suggested instructions, of which there was no lack, harped upon a frank and open administration of Indian affairs, the chief theme of which was to be rigid economy. Gage wrote in transmitting the major his appointment:

I can't recommend to you too strongly the strictest economy in the small expenses that may unavoidably be incurred at your post. Nothing new or chargeable must on any account be done by you upon your own head.[7]

6. *Johnson Mss.*, 13, 22.
7. *Johnson Mss.*, 12, 10.

Rogers was further informed that in all his dealings with the savages he must pay the strictest obedience to Johnson, and report as frequently to him as to the military commandant at Detroit. In June, again, supplementary instructions were issued to him from Johnson Hall, cautioning him, as Indian commissary, to acquaint himself with the tribes, to avoid giving them any umbrage, and to see that his garrison and the traders committed no offense; and, above all, to send in exact copies of all his proceedings to headquarters, under affidavit, every six months.[8]

Finally, Johnson took opportunity to hold a long and earnest conference with him, giving him minutely detailed instructions as to his conduct toward the Indians, while Gage did as much for military affairs; and both, "finding him very desirous of some liberty in the article of expenses," cautioned him thoroughly again to avoid useless expenditures.

Throughout the spring of 1766 Johnson was still pushing his new plan regarding Indian affairs; and finally, by a bold step, he determined upon its inauguration. He knew that in this he was as yet supported by scant authority from England; but Gage approved and abetted his conduct, and to him the temper of the Indians and the ominous movements of the French and Spanish on the Mississippi made the step seem imperative. The French *habitants* on the Missouri, Mississippi, Illinois, and Miami, as he pointed out, monopolized most of the trade in those parts; for despite the fact that they could procure goods only at great expense, the sensitive western tribesmen would go on long journeys in order to barter their furs for powder, tobacco, and cloth with those who would treat with them kindly, courteously, and fairly, and not as a debased, inferior people. Yet while he acknowledged that he could never persuade the English to offer the savages more than a polite civility, Johnson was far from despairing of weakening the French influence through his commissaries. These men were to ingratiate themselves into the favour of the tribes, by presents and cajolery; were to supervise the various traders who made the posts their headquarters, and—putting a

---

8. *P. R. O., C. O. 5,* Vol. 85, p. 351.

stop to their dishonesty and cruelty—to force them to pay fair prices, to be considerate and gentle, and to stop their pernicious traffic in rum; and were to nip all plots or discontents in the bud, and counteract directly all foreign influences. Johnson wrote to London in January, 1766:

I have for some time made choice of the best persons for these offices at all the posts, and no time may be lost after I receive orders to appoint them.

Meanwhile he had called Pontiac and all the chiefs of the west to a conference at Oswego, to announce his new plan.[9] Finally, on March 22, he wrote the Board of Trade that he was on the eve of making the necessary proposed appointments, although he was not yet for some weeks to announce them.[10] "I hope your lordship will not disapprove of my conduct," he added, and suggested that they might infer its urgency from the fact that the appointments would be made at risk of his private fortune. His mails from that day onward were choked with applications. The great significance of his move was clear. It meant that henceforth the government of the west and north was not to be purely military, but half-military and half civil, and that he and Gage would divide its authority. For almost a year murmurs of subordinate jealousy from western military officers had greeted the proposal, and now the moment for real friction was at hand.

For a short period during the spring Rogers was at home at Portsmouth; and here his wife, not yet fully estranged from him, decided to accompany him to his distant command. The unhappy woman was urged by many friends, in sincere remonstrance, to refrain from a step which, no less from the character of the major than from the location of the post, was full of uncertainty and danger. Her father, however, animated by a Puritan churchman's sense of duty, exhorted her to perform the full tenor of her vows, and she herself "felt some hope yet of winning her husband by gentleness and condescension."[11]

9. *Documents Relative to the Colonial History of New York*, VII, 808 ff.

10. *Documents Relative to the Colonial History of New York*, VII, 817.

11. Elizabeth Rogers' Petition of February 11th, 1778, to the New Hampshire assembly.

Accompanied by her, therefore, Rogers set out in June, under orders from Johnson to proceed to Oswego, and take charge there of the preparations for the impending congress of the western Indians. Here, at the little fort and village planted at the mouth of Oswego River, were now gathering the chiefs of the Potawatomi, Huron, and Chippewa, and the principal men of the Ottawa, all anxiously awaiting the coming of Pontiac, their leader and most accomplished diplomatist, who since the failure of his conspiracy had been a wanderer in the Illinois country.

On the English side the chief representatives were to be, besides Johnson and Rogers, Daniel Claus, head of Indian affairs in the province of Quebec, Edward Cole, newly appointed commissary at Fort de Chartres, Jehu Hay, holding the same office at Detroit, and—most interesting of all—Lieutenant Benjamin Roberts, one of Johnson's most trusted aids, and commissary at Oswego since the preceding April.[12] The meeting of the major with this last officer, already of course on the spot, was curiously watched, for it was rumoured that the commissary was soon to be sent out to Mackinac to take over a share of Rogers' responsibility in Indian relations, and there were many points in the temperament of each that seemed prophetic of a clash between them.

Roberts was an experienced English officer, still young, who had been with Rogers' corps in 1757, and had participated in many of the most fatiguing expeditions. His zeal in ingratiating himself with the Indians had first recommended him to Johnson's notice. He early learned the Mohawk language, and because of this, and a very curious incident, the savages of New York took a violent fancy to him.[13] While at garrison at Schenectady in 1759, the gentlemen and ladies acted *Othello*, before an audience room crowded with chiefs and braves, most of whom were wrought up to an extraordinary pitch of curiosity. The gallantly attired Roberts strutted upon the stage as Lodovico, saluted by a fanfare of trumpets, and responding to a general burst of accla-

12. *Documents Relative to the Colonial History of New York*, VII, 850 ff.
13. This biographical material is drawn from two long petitions of Roberts', dated May 27th and June 9th, 1773, among the unpublished *Dartmouth Mss.*

mations by repeatedly doffing a hat of truly Venetian courtliness The Indians were so much struck by his general appearance, especially by his plumed headpiece, that they concluded him to be a personage of exalted importance; and he confirmed their awed admiration by giving them both his hat and velvet cloak, for which they could not be sufficiently grateful.

In the last years of the war he served at Fort Stanwix, near Niagara. Everywhere and always he flattered the Indians; everywhere he mastered their dialect; everywhere he acquainted himself with their customs and temper. He even reconciled himself to marrying an influential old squaw, a virago of whom he spoke as one of the most frightful of human beings. In 1766, when his regiment was ordered back to England, Johnson stopped him to engage him in "settling disputes between the western Indians and the Six Nations, and to help regulate the Indian trade."

He was an intimate and a favourite of Johnson's; a faithful, sincere officer, and an ardent partisan of those with whom his interest was enlisted. His zeal in military and tribal matters had involved him heavily in debt, from which, however, he was unwilling to extricate himself by unprincipled means. With all his fine moral temper and efficient conscientiousness there seems to have been intermixed a heavy streak of impulsiveness and emotionalism. A rude, frank, impatient man like Rogers was sure to seem dangerous to him, just as Roberts had seemed troublesome and pettish to many of his superiors.

With everything in tension at the little fort for the coming conference, at which Pontiac was expected to give in his adherence to British rule, the two men were not long in quarrelling. The major seized the reins of affairs officiously, for his military jealousy of the commissary was not diminished by the report that such a faithful servant of Johnson Hall was likely soon to become his co-worker at his new post; and the brusqueness with which he treated Roberts soon had its upshot in a sharp quarrel as to their respective powers.[14]

At the mouth of the Oswego River, and on its farther shore,

14. *Johnson Mss.*, 13, 93.

Captain Peeke Fuller of the post had tentatively stationed a number of traders. Their position there was in accordance with the wishes of Johnson, as local conditions made it possible to control their trade more effectually on that side; for military reasons, however, Rogers set about transferring them to a point near the walls of the fort. When Roberts protested, he was peremptorily silenced, and his quotation of Johnson's authority availed naught. The controversy grew into one in which Rogers refused decisively to respect Johnson's general orders that his commissaries were to be obeyed in all affairs pertaining to the trade. "He thinks," wrote the humiliated Roberts, "that he is not to obey all orders that do not come directly from the general."[15]

Petty in itself, the incident showed the determination of the newly-appointed governor to assert his independence as a military commandant, even against the authority of Sir William; and it is significant as the beginning of his relations with one who was later his chief enemy.

The congress with the Indians began July 23rd, in the shade of some magnificent trees between the river and the parade-ground of the fort, and endured three days. The temper of the savages at the moment demanded immediate appeasal. Johnson wrote:

> The injuries and slights they have met with give us no room to upbraid them. Our people on the frontier seem determined to bring on a new war in the face of their own ruin. Twenty murders upon them have been treacherously committed within the six months past.[16]

He represented himself as at his wits end for means to stop the provocations of the whites, and urged constantly upon the home government the clothing of the commissaries with new power.

> I cannot check their grievances and the commissaries are in the same situation. They have an office and a duty laid down for them, but no power to execute it. To answer the purposes of the appointment they must be empowered to see commerce equitably conducted, and justice executed.

15. *Johnson Mss.*, 12, 232.
16. *Documents Relative to the Colonial History of New York*, VII, 851.

His querulous plea arose, doubtless, in part from such instances as Rogers' disrespectful handling of Roberts. Yet he spoke boldly to the Indians of the new scheme, as well as of the measures for checking the outrages of frontier farmers along the Alleghenies.

"You begin already," he addressed them, "to see and feel the fruits of peace, from the number of traders and plenty of goods at all our garrisoned posts, and are enjoying the peaceable possession of Illinois. You will likewise now see that proper officers, men of honour and probity, are appointed to reside at the posts, to prevent abuses in trade."

He exhorted them to confine their commerce to the forts, pointing out the impossibility of checking fraud if they refused. To all this the Indians gravely bowed.

"We heartily thank you, father, for having appointed the commissaries, and for not letting the traders straggle through the woods to our villages, but to trade only at the posts; it was not prudent to let them ramble where they pleased, but there will be no danger along the waters to the forts, and we shall be justly dealt with," said Tiata, chief of the Huron, and all promised their furtherance of the plan, accepting it as an earnest of the love of the English people.[17] After further parley, and Pontiac's final submission, the congress broke up to general satisfaction.

In the early days of August, Rogers and his wife, with Rogers secretary Potter, arrived at Mackinac, having come through by way of Niagara, Detroit, and the lakes. The post stood then on a bold point a mile or two west of the present site of Mackinac city, just south of and overlooking the straits; and to arrive at it Rogers passed the beautiful Mackinac Island, its high, blanched limestone cliffs, crowned and backed by heavy pine forests, rising in irregular splendour from the lake.

Newly rebuilt since Pontiac's war, the fort was not a prepossessing structure, for it was neither commodious nor strong; and its situation, among monotonous sand-dunes that ran back for a long distance before they were broken by the odorous

---

17. *Documents Relative to the Colonial History of New York*, VII, 854.

woods of cedar and pine, was bleak in winter and baking hot in summer. Heavy barracks rose near the fort proper, and at some distance stood the French village of Mackinac, a cluster of white-plastered log houses, defining the extremities of the long, narrow, rectangular plot in which the villagers cultivated their land. In front—the opposite shore outlined by well-wooded heights—spread the brief straits, widening away on either hand into the lovely waters of Huron and Michigan. The little garrison numbered two companies,[18] and Captain Spiessmacher, a German officer at its head, resigned the position of chief command into Rogers' hands.

The latter installed himself within the most comfortable of the officers' houses within the stockade walls, and set himself to gaining a full acquaintanceship with his new duties and opportunities. He had left Roberts behind at Niagara, and. except for his ironclad oral and written instructions, he was invested with full powers as commander of the garrison and agent of Indian affairs. With a full appreciation of the isolation of his post—for Detroit was a long week's journey behind him, and a rigorous winter, which would stop all communication with the east, but a few months away—his feeling was one of autocratic independence. Except for his instructions from Gage and Johnson, which he now might with temporary security entirely disregard, his own affairs and those of the region were under the direct guidance of his hand. He could undertake whatever ambitious administrative schemes he deemed best, and—if fair fortune offered—attempt a replenishment of his exhausted purse, free from all but the most distant supervision. From his temper and his previous financial irresponsibility it was clear he would not halt at heavy bills when impressed with the opportunity of carrying through some striking, largely-conceived scheme; and that in affairs with the tribes he would regard himself as chiefly responsible to Gage, and would order matters of trade and of Indian relations with but scant deference to Johnson.

This last, indeed, was immediately evident. Johnson had

18. *P. R. O., C. O.* 5,Vol. 85, p. 155.

given to Rogers, as to all the commissaries, strictest orders that the Indian trade was to be confined to the immediate vicinity of the fort; that the packs of the dealers were to be opened, as far as possible, only under the commandants eyes; that no cheating was to be allowed, and a fixed scale of prices, which Johnson, himself scheduled, was to be enforced; and that the commandant should control jealously the entire issuance of rum to the Indians. The general order was clearly repugnant to one who, like Rogers, knew intimately the circumstances under which the traffic in furs went on in the north-west. Ever since the foundation of the fur trade by the French *coureurs-de-bois* the tribes of the region had parted with their peltry on the very hunting-ground upon which they did their winter shooting and trapping. The market had been an itinerant one; and following the various villages of braves into the snowy wilderness each winter, the French adventurer, with his cloth, trinkets, liquor, hatchets, guns, grease, and provisions of powder and shot, had saved them the necessity of interrupting their hunts for a long, exhausting trip, over choked trails, to a central depot of stores. Adopting the Indian's ways, learning even his dialect, by tact and kindliness reaching his very heart, the wandering trader would sleep at night in his *wigwam*, warm himself by his fire, eat at his rude board, and, indeed, make himself a member of the savage community. He had a supply of exchangeable goods always in the sight of the eager tribesmen, who knew the sole commodity by the barter of which they could procure any desired article, and set themselves to secure it; he could give them necessities, as of weapons, or ammunition, or tools, on the spot; he could save them the occasion of leaving their wives and children a prey to starvation, and their country to hostile tribes, while they carried their growing packs in to market. More than that, he could penetrate to far-off peoples, and bring back bundles of fur that else would never have touched a Caucasian hand. Far beyond the pioneer clearing, far beyond the garrison, he was the real *vidette* of commerce and civilization. Rogers knew that to keep the traders under the walls of his fort would cut in half the commercial importance of Mackinac, and he lost no time in resolving to disobey Johnson's injunction. Immediately upon his arrival he issued a general permit to all traders to "go wintering," and follow the Indians along their trails to the coverts of the lynx, the mink, and the beaver. "For this," wrote the indignant Daniel Claus, superintendent of the district, from Montreal, "he is vastly liked and applauded here."[19]

The approbation of Montreal was indeed fervent. In the merchant houses of that city centred almost all the channels of trade which drained the Mackinac district. Trafficking in old French fashion, and with their factors on every trail in Ontario and Michigan, these firms had been the earliest and most active in their opposition to Johnson's plan. They foresaw that their agents at Oswego, Niagara, Detroit, and above all at Mackinac, dealing with peoples who for generations to them almost immemorial had sold from the hunting lodge and thicket, would be ruined by the new policy. They had not contented themselves with direct protests to Johnson; they had instructed the Indians of the west and north to send in pleas that each of their multitudinous villages along the Illinois, Wisconsin, Saguenay, and Ottawa might be allowed a trader, pleas that multiplied throughout 1765 and 1766, and they had induced a large number of the inhabitants of Montreal to sign a petition presented to the lords of trade in May, 1766, setting forth the incalculable damage being wrought the commerce of his majesty's subjects by the new regulations, and praying for a redress.[20]

Pressure had been brought, too, upon Rogers predecessor, Captain Howard, who had been constrained by clamour and influence to release a number of the traders from the most irksome of the restrictions; so that the majors decisive step had not been without its indecisive precedent. Johnson had protested most vigorously, however, at the course of Howard, who had been saved from a severe visitation of official wrath

19. *Johnson Mss.*, 13, 134.
20. *Documents Relative to the Colonial History of New York*, VII, 871.

only by the recall which installed Rogers in his stead. Now the latter, by letting not merely several, but all of the traders, go *en bivernement*, had placed himself in the full path of the Indian commissioner's biting anger. This he knew so fully that he may well have been guided in his complaisance toward certain of the factors by interested motives.

Rogers, indeed, began fast to make friends about the fort; and we know, from the records concerning the latter part of his administration, the names of the more important of these, all men interested in the trade: Atkinson, Goddard, Stuart, Des Rivieres, and Tute, the last—named a New Hampshire neighbour with whom Rogers had had business dealings three years before.[21] The most memorable of his relationships at the inception of his duties, however, was with a needy adventurer who had followed him out from the east upon a previous understanding—Jonathan Carver.

This officer, slightly older than Rogers, had first come into contact with the leader of the rangers in the fighting about Lake George, where he also had served as a provincial captain.[22] He was a native of Connecticut, born, like Rogers, into a frontier community, and left fatherless at an even earlier age, though amid surroundings vastly better for his education. Wounded at the massacre of Fort William Henry, he had written a vivid and stirring account of that sorry occurrence. He was retired

---

21. See various deeds kept at the office of the secretary of state in Concord, New Hampshire. Tute had also served as a lieutenant in the rangers under Rogers in the Seven Years War and was captured while on a scout from Fort Edward in 1760; Rogers *Journals*. He was one of Rogers' most trusted friends and agents. Stuart also had been an adjutant in the rangers under Rogers. James Stanley Goddard was one of the earliest traders from Montreal in the upper country, and in 1761 was operating from Mackinac and Green Bay. After Pontiac's conspiracy he became one of the most prominent merchants in the north-west, and Claus wrote Johnson in 1768 that he had more influence among the Indians there than any other single man. In 1777 he was commissioned general storekeeper for the government, at Montreal, a position which he held as late as 1795. In 1767 Carver named a river emptying into Lake Superior after him. Johnson Mss., 16, 134. Wisconsin Historical Coll., XVIII, 285; Carver's *Travels*.

22. This information is most largely drawn from petitions of Carver's presented to the Board of Trade when he went to England in 1769 to secure his expenses for his journey; see *Board of Trade, Commercial Papers*, Volume 459.

from the service in 1763, returning to Massachusetts, where his company had been raised, and apparently dragging out a rather painful civil existence there for the next two years. Now, in the middle of August, he was at Mackinac, head bent with the major over vast plans which centred about one wild surmise.

In one way, perhaps through hearing of Rogers' petition of 1765, more probably through meeting him upon his return from London, Carver had been struck with the possibility of aiding the governor of Mackinac in carrying out, upon a modest scale, his glorious scheme for the discovery of the semi-fabulous Northwest Passage. In his published travels he long after attempted to arrogate to himself the credit for his expedition,[23] saying that he was independently struck by the possibility in it of performing a further service to the king; but it has already been shown that Rogers had made a similar proposal to the ministry in 1765, so that he has a better claim to be the originator of the plan.[24] Carver's missions would have in his own ambitions an almost inexplicable origin; he must have known that he, a landless, almost penniless officer, could never have financed it; and if he had conceived it alone it is unbelievable that he would not have sought some official approbation for it.

Three years later in London, at the very moment Rogers was collecting his personal expenses in the expedition, Carver'secured his own share by swearing before the privy council for plantation affairs that it was only in consequence of the governor's commission that he undertook the journey.[25]

---

23. *Travels Through the Interior Part of North America,* by J. Carver, London, 1779.
24. There has been a very considerable reaction from the complete condemnation of Carver's *Travels,* since the publication of E. C. Bourne's destructive criticism, *American Historical Review,* XI, 2, p. 287. The study of Carver's career by John T. Lee in the Wisconsin Historical Society's *Proceedings,* 1912, pp. 87-123, *Ibid,* 1909, pp. 143-153, has completely overthrown most of Professor Bourne's contentions, and, as far as his actual travels are concerned, Carver 15 regarded today by historians as a reliable witness. See also M. M. Quaife, *The Evolution of Source Material for Western History,* in *Mississippi Valley Historical Review,* I, 167 and following (September, 1914). It is interesting to note that for Carver's descriptions of the beaver, bear, and porcupine, pp. 282, 274, and 279 of the *Travels,* he drew almost verbatim upon Rogers paragraphs upon the same, pp. 253, 259, and 263 of the *Concise Account.*
25. *Board of Trade, Commercial Papers,* Volume 459.

Finally, we gather from a letter of Claus' to Johnson that Rogers had returned from England still quite full of the plan he had broached there—so full that he was willing to seize the opportunity his new authority gave him.[26] The enterprise was rapidly put under way. In June, while Rogers was in New England or New York, Carver set out from Boston, and taking the same ship as his superior,[27] apparently arrived with him, or at any rate not many days behind him, at the straits, thirteen hundred miles to the west. The prompt assistance which the major, so new at his post, rendered him, far beyond the measures of his legal powers, is almost indubitable evidence of previous collusion. On August 12th Rogers issued Carver a commission as leader of a special exploring detail from the fort, at a salary of eight shillings daily, "for the purpose of making surveys of

26. *Johnson Mss.,* 16, 134. Claus speaks of Lieutenant Pauli of the Royal Americans having proposed to him in confidence a plan for an expedition northwest of Lake Superior, "he having made himself acquainted with the discoveries of several nations at sea, particularly those of the Russians, which latter gave him great encouragement," and compares Pauli's fitness for the journey with that of Rogers, as the originator of an earlier and similar scheme, which Rogers was still hopeful of carrying out.

27. It seems impossible to determine just when or how Carver arrived at Mackinac; for deliberately or otherwise, his *Travels* throw a great deal of dust about those of his movements which immediately preceded the initiation of his expedition. In 1700 the only schooner plying between Detroit and Mackinac was the *Gladwin* which had played such a part in the siege of Detroit: if he arrived upon it he almost certainly came with Rogers, for trips were infrequent, and he was at the post early in August. He may, however, have come by canoe. It may as well be remarked here as anywhere, that throughout his book Carver seems anxious to exclude Rogers' name from any connection with his travels, and makes no mention whatever of him in narrating his return to Mackinac at the end of the summer of 1767. He speaks merely of the tranquil pleasures of fishing and of the passing of the time in pleasant company, during the stirring months in which Rogers was arrested, kept in irons, and the entire settlement was full of excitement. In a letter from the fort to his wife, September 24, 1767, he states that the date of his arrival was August 30; while in his *Travels* he puts it "at the beginning of November." In this letter he further says that "on my return to this place, I received the thanks of the governor commandant, who has promised he will take special care to acquaint the government at home of my services," and that "I have two hundred pounds sterling due to me from the crown, which I shall have in the spring." Published by John T. Lee in Wisconsin Historical Society *Proceedings,* 1909, p. 149, and in *The Nation,* New York, Volume XCIX, 161. Carver returned to his family at Montague, Massachusetts, in August, 1769.

the interior, especially to the west and northwest, and outlining carefully the route to be followed."[28]

He endowed Carver and his companions liberally with supplies, promised to send more to the Falls of St. Anthony, and advised him as carefully as his superior knowledge of the Indians and the west warranted him. The hopes and fears of both officers were high. If the exploration succeeded in even a portion of its objects it would benefit both immeasurably. The west, in all its rich resources, its scenery, and its Indian life, was unknown; its plains, rivers, mountains, unmapped; the routes to the western ocean but conjectural. To penetrate it would be at once to confer a benefit upon science and geography, to give England a claim to its possession, to open it to settlement, and perhaps, if a water passage above the "Ouragon" did not prove mythical, to give a new impulse to commerce. On the third day of September, Carver set forth with several traders and guides down Lake Michigan. The trip was destined to do much less, and much more, than was expected of it; it was to discover no Northwest Passage, and to map no vast extent of unknown territory; but it was to give birth to a book of travel which should arouse European curiosity for America as no other ever had, and to interest Schiller, Chateaubriand, and Byron.[29] As stout paddlers drove the canoes out over the choppy waters of the straits, the cheers of the garrison bade the explorers farewell. Before they returned affairs at the fort were to undergo a momentous revolution.

---

28. *Board of Trade, Commercial Papers,* Volume 459. Carver says he never received the provisions which Rogers promised to send him to the Falls of St. Anthony; but it is certain that they were sent to him, for Rogers was later paid for them. The fact that Carver used that part of Rogers plan of 1765 which appointed the falls as headquarters for the first winter may have a slight significance. See Carver's Petition of Feb. 10th, 1773, in the *Earl of Dartmouth's Mss.*

29. In evidence of the astonishing popularity of Carver's *Travels* John T. Lee enumerates thirty editions, with translations into German, French, and Dutch. (Wisconsin Historical Society Proceedings, 1909, pp. 143-183.) "From Carver's *Travels* Chateaubriand drew not a few of the descriptions of Indian customs for his fascinating and poetic *Voyage en Amerique.* From the same source Schiller derived the language and thought for his Nadowessier's Todtenlied, familiar to English readers through Bulwer-Lytton's translation as *The Indian s Death Dirge.*" Joseph Bedier, *Etudes Critiques*, Paris, 1903, on Chateaubriand.

During the autumn and early winter Rogers continued his government in the most ambitious fashion. His chief concern, after granting the traders their desired immunity from Johnson's rules, was to secure the favour and friendship of the tribes of the north-west. The Indians in the vicinity of the fort he immediately found means of pleasing. The same traders that rejoiced Montreal and angered Claus with their reports of Rogers' freedom with the trade brought news also that his behaviour toward the Indians was liked and approved by them, as well as the people of Mackinac.[30] Generosity, flattery, and a liberality of fair promises characterized his treatment of his red children. But to gain the golden opinions of those near the fort, while he merely indulged the others with traders, did not satisfy him.

Only a few weeks after his arrival, therefore, he sent forth an embassy among the faraway Folles Avoines, Puan, Saux, Renard, Chippewa, and Sioux, under Goddard and Des Rivieres, ostensibly to notify them of his assumption of the command of Mackinac, of the concluding of peace between Pontiac and the English, and of the occupation of Illinois.[31] The dwellings of these tribes were scattered over the great distances of Wisconsin, Michigan, northern Illinois, and even the immediate trans-Mississippi region; but the undaunted embassy loaded itself for its long journey with numerous presents. Despite all the cautions he had received, Rogers succeeded in spending £300 in Indian affairs within the first six weeks after his arrival, and duly drew a draft for this amount upon Johnson.[32] Moreover, his disbursements continued to be heavy. The great tribe of the Chippewa, residing for the most part above the Ottawa river and north and west along Lake Superior, were threatening a war with the Sioux, and were trying to involve in it their allies, the Ottawas and Pottawattomies, both Michigan tribes. This

---

30. *Johnson Mss.*, 13, 134.
31. *Documents Relative to the Colonial History of New York*, VII, 989. *Documentary History of New York*, II, 863. *Johnson Mss.*, 15, 125; 13: 74 and 89. Near the St. Croix River in November, 1766, Carver mediated a peace between the Sioux and a band of hostile Chippewa.
32. *Documentary History of New York*, II, 848. *Johnson Mss.*, 13: 74 and 89.

conflict Rogers laboured anxiously to prevent, fearing that it would disrupt the whole western trade; and his protests to the chiefs he again enforced by expensive presents.[33]

His messengers he kept out all winter, and he even found means to intercept roving bands of tribesmen, whom he conciliated over-generously. By Christmas his expenditures had necessitated a second draft on Johnson for about £500, with more immediately to follow.[34]

Simultaneously Rogers was becoming personally much entangled, and deeply dissipated. Most of the goods for his lavish gifts he had secured on credit from the favourably impressed and over-confident traders, representing Montreal and English firms;[35] so large was the stock advanced him he may even have hoped to engage in the trade himself, through clandestine agents. As time passed, the merchants, who had at first hoped for exorbitant prices, realized that Rogers' extravagant course would so embroil him with Johnson that they might receive nothing at all, while they also began to fear an overt motive in his zealous conciliation of the tribes; and they entered upon a course of constant harassing and importunity.

The commander gave way, too, to a course of sustained licentiousness, no whit mitigated by his wife's restraining presence. His chief vices, probably learned in London, attacked him with extreme vigour during the long winter season, the enforced confinement of which told much upon his nervous, energetic spirit. When for months the ice, piling at times sixty feet high in the straits outside, cut off all navigation, and the town and fort lay snowbound and isolated between the wilderness and the lake, his constant recourse was to carouse in the garrison or village, with companions of the most doubtful cast. His sensitive

---

33. See *Documents Relative to the Colonial History of New York*, VII, 966, 969 (where Johnson says the expense incurred on this head "contrary to orders within a few months amounts to several thousand pounds, apparently to serve the interests of a few traders"), 989. *Johnson Mss.*, 15, 26.

34. *Johnson Mss.*, 14, 42.

35. *Johnson Mss.*, 18: 185, 186; 19: 112, 163, 172, 179, 185, 226. Treasury Minutes, February, 1772. In *Johnson Mss.*, 14, 193, is given a bill of Stephen Groesbeck for goods given by Rogers to the Indian nations at Mackinac.

wife suffered deeply from his conduct, while her grief was supplemented by a sense of the certain gulf to which his improvidence and disobedience of orders was leading him. She says:

> To paint in their true colours my sufferings during my stay in that remote and lonely region would be a task beyond my ability. It is enough to say that I underwent every hardship, and endured every species of ill-treatment which infidelity, uncleanness, and drunken barbarity could inflict.

Thus the winter passed away; and when, along with reports of his disregard of instructions, along with his rapidly mounting drafts, there reached Johnson rumours of his dissipation and his debts, it was determined to send Roberts, still commissary at Niagara, on to Mackinac. Worst of all, the drafts were decisively, if temporarily, refused payment by Johnson, upon the ground that he "had no letter of advice from any person upon the subject," and peremptory orders were sent to Rogers to incur no more expenses.[36]

Roberts, who by Johnsons orders, Gage concurring, was ready to start for Mackinac from Oswego late in April, was delayed by various circumstances, and did not reach his destination until June 23, 1768.[37] In the interim Rogers continued his eccentric and arbitrary conduct of affairs. In the early spring he sent his assistant, Potter, upon an expedition to the upper reaches of Lake Superior, to continue treating with the still warlike Chippewa.[38] It was observed about the fort at the time that his manner was becoming more discontented and restless than ever; a fact traced to his increasing debts, and the embarrassment caused him by the refusal of his drafts upon the government.

In the closing days of winter he threw himself secretly into the formulation of a new and amazing scheme, which—a last gleam of hope for his material salvation—was designed to render more direct his control over the region, to stimulate the fur trade, and

---

36. *Documentary History of New York*, II, 848, 853, 863, 865.
37. The chief of these circumstances was the failure of Captain McLeod to take his place promptly at Niagara.
38. *Documents Relative to the Colonial History of New York*, VII, 990.

to make him forever independent of his troublesome eastern superiors. This was a proposal for a new form of government at Mackinac, which we find drawn up in formal detail in a petition transmitted direct to the Board of Trade on May 29th, 1768.[39] An effective preamble attacked Johnson's restrictions and recited the vast extent of the fur trade at Mackinac, the exchangeable value of which was declared to reach £60,000, or one hundred heavy boat-loads of Montreal goods, yearly; the circumstances which proved that even this volume of trade, if properly nourished, could be immensely increased; and the fact that Mackinac, with its commanding situation on three lakes, stood as the logical centre for the entire north-west.

Rogers wished, therefore, to have established at Mackinac a combined civil and military government which should give a more direct attention to Indian affairs, and feel a more sincere anxiety as to means of controlling and developing traffic possessing many local and peculiar characteristics. He asked to be appointed governor, with power of electing one of his subordinate officers as lieutenant-governor, and another secretary; while the rest of his plan embraced a council of twelve, to be chosen by popular vote from among the citizens of the town, with limited legislative and advisory functions.

To preserve order he wished a few companies of rangers, ready to enforce his mandates among all the French or savage inhabitants of the whole vast territory; and he craved allowance of—

.... a fixed sum annually, for presents to keep the Indians peaceable—such as shall be thought adequate for a post to which more than one third the Indians on the continent resort, beside other nations as far as the Pacific.

Like the governor of a crown colony, he was to be responsible only to the king's ministers. The plan was suggestive, but its

---

39. This petition contains more than six thousand words, and is phrased as carefully as it is planned. As Potter himself is authority for the statement that it was composed secretly by Rogers, and during Potter's own absence, the document alone is sufficient to refute Johnson's allegation that Rogers was illiterate. Johnson composed a long reply to it (*Documents Relative to the Colonial History of New York*, VII, 997).

obvious inspiration lay in his debts, his troubles with the traders and with Johnson, and the increasing certainty that a commissary would soon be watchfully at his side. It was clear that, under a scheme for promoting trade, he was virtually proposing that he be given the most absolute control over the tribes, the fur business, the garrison of the north-west, and a large sum of money.

As his negotiations with the tribes progressed, Rogers kept his agents, with their presents, still out among the villages, and himself visited a number of the chiefs. He had issued a call for a general convocation of the tribes in June, and as the war clouds that hung over the Sioux and the Chippewa drew off, it became evident that this would be one of the most impressive gatherings of savages ever held on the American continent. His messengers, from far beyond the Wisconsin, and down the Mississippi, brought back news that the most distant prairies were sending their braves.[40] The ostensible object of the gathering was the final ratification of the Sioux-Chippewa peace, and as such was deeply irritating to Johnson from the very moment he heard of it. "It is not good policy," he objected, "to interest ourselves in quarrels of distant nations, which do not affect our forts, settlements, or communications. It may indeed be interesting to a dozen traders, who in defiance of all orders go to the Indian towns; but on the other hand these wars take off and engage some of the most violent of the Indians, who would otherwise be dangerous to us. Above all, it was a most expensive affair.[41]

Between May 26th and June 10th a vast concourse of Indians, comprising many of the *sachems* and braves of the Ottawa, Potawatomi, Chippewa, Nascapee and Missisaugus, began pouring

40. When Carver returned south-eastward in April, 1767, from wintering among the Sioux, to secure provisions, he was accompanied by a large band of tribesmen whom he persuaded to go on before him to the great conference at Mackinac, while he himself struck off toward Prairie du Chien. See *Travels*. Tute was credited at this time with "carrying matters with a high hand on the Mississippi, giving gorgets to the Indians inscribed with *fleurs-de-lis*, and creating numerous chiefs." *Johnson Mss.*, 15, 125. Goddard and others were similarly busy; and of Goddard it was written, "they have found out the river that runs from Lake Superior to the Mississippi. *Wisconsin Historical Collections*, XVIII, 285.
41. *New York Colonial Documents*, VII, 969. Johnson regarded the peace as a pretext of Rogers "to acquire a name and influence among the Indians for his purposes." Idem, p. 989.

in toward the straits. Rogers, with his able lieutenants, Tute and Goddard, the latter of whom had unbounded influence with the aborigines, marshalled them into order, and kept them quiet.[42]

On June 24th the Sioux, Saux, Folles Avoines, Puan, and Renard, accompanied by a band of fresh Ottawa as protectors from the still churlish Chippewa, arrived in such numbers that the waters of the lake were blackened by their canoes. The woods for a great distance about were filled with their tents, and through the forest paths and over the sandy shingle roamed one of the most picturesque and motley assemblages in Indian history.

For a time minor conferences were held. Finally, on July 3rd, in the shade beside the lake, all the tribes gathered in one great and dignified convention, friendly and disaffected side by side, and the chiefs interchanged assurances of friendship and love, united in protesting their loyalty to the English, and passed about a huge *calumet*. Even the Sioux, after recounting that "the Chippewa have lately stained our country with blood, and given us great provocation to lift up the hatchet against them," promised forbearance until Rogers, "our father next to the great king," redressed their injuries. They all delighted Rogers by begging that they might have traders sent among them.

Before the meeting broke up, the governor devoted one whole day to the distribution of many presents, secured upon more drafts from the merchants of the town. With these the red men departed rejoicing. Their congress had been a splendid and unforgettable pageant, and had inspired them with some fealty to the British Empire; but the piper was still to be paid.

The bills incurred in these conferences were promptly presented to Johnson by eastern agents of the Mackinac merchants, and as promptly roused him to a high pitch of anger. Despite the fact that other commissaries, notably Cole of Fort de Chartres, had recently sent in requests for sums which were, says Johnson, "vastly more than I could have thought of," he considered Rogers' expenditures wholly unjustifiable. As presented during the

---

42. Rogers has left a circumstantial account of this conference, in a paper entitled *The Journal of Major Rogers, May 24th–July 23rd, 1767,* which is preserved in the library of the American Antiquarian Society, Worcester, Massachusetts.

summer in Montreal and Albany, they reached a grand total of £5000.[43] His suspicions equalled his resentment. He was at once certain that Rogers had been meddling with Indian affairs in a wholly unwarrantable way, and with a design to further his own overweening ambitions; he wrote Gage:

> There must be some particular motive for this. Expenses seem to have been made, Indians called, and traders indulged purely to procure their esteem.

All in all, he was ready at once to demand Rogers immediate recall. Meanwhile, on June 23rd, Roberts had taken office at Mackinac, with instructions to cut down expenses, to watch Rogers, and to enforce the trade regulations. He was received with so plain a show of jealousy and bad feeling that none of his three tasks was easy.[44]

The commandant attempted from the very beginning to throw difficulties in his way; to increase his expenses, prejudice the traders against him, and to render impossible full obedience to Johnson. Indeed, Roberts' reports indicated that from the very first he was troubled both by the plain irregularities about the post, and the commandant's obvious intention of increasing the friction incident upon maintaining order among the traders. In his first letter to Johnson he showed that many merchants were plying their art away from the post, and beyond his powers of supervision; that Rogers was trying to betray him into extravagance; that he was covertly attempting to secure from the Indians a petition for Roberts' withdrawal, and his own restoration to full control; and that rum sometimes got among the savages. He pointed out, too, a dangerous tendency among the soldiery to participate in the trade, to forestall which he recommended a frequent relief of the garrison.

---

43. *Documentary History of New York*, II, 863. September 6th, 1767, he says: "On my arrival at Albany I was surrounded by people with drafts drawn on me by Major Rogers, to between £2000 and £3000." September 11th, "Further drafts on me have been shown at Montreal to the amount of £1100, and I hear the whole exceeds £5000." All these bills were at once protested. *Idem*, 865.

44. *Documentary History of New York*, II, 864. The date of Roberts' arrival is noted on a *Return of the Trade at Mackinac, Dartmouth Mss.*; dated 1767.

In his plan for the civil government of Mackinac, indeed, Rogers had given open indication of the nature of his preference among the traders of the region; he had declared:

Since it is true that the French at Mackinac, St. Mary's, Green Bay, and other places where they are looking and walking up and down, are an indolent slothful set of vagabonds, ill disposed to the English and very influential among the savages, ought they not for the better security of the *British* trade to be removed out of the country?[45]

To men like Tute, Goddard, Engineer, and Atherton he tried constantly to divert the trade, employing them at times as his direct agents among the tribes, and at times allowing them full freedom in their own commercial transactions. Roberts described such men as—

. . . . simple, canting, over-reaching New Englanders, who watch every opportunity of making the Indians drunk, and cheating them of their furs, continually abuse one another, and never speak well of anyone in power.[46]

Whatever may have been their attitude toward the Indians, and toward Spiessmacher and the commissary, they were evidently bound by the closest ties of self-interest to each other and to Rogers. Their primary interest was undoubtedly commercial, and the perpetuation of their advantages by the thwarting of Roberts' strict and suspicious policy.

The obstacles in Roberts' way multiplied as the weeks went on; yet by conscientious labour he began slowly to triumph over them. Throughout the long summer days, when the lazy Indians lounged in throngs in the woods and camps about the straits, a fertile soil for the corruptions and wiles of the villagers, his chief fear was that the traders might carry rum among them, and so inflame them to violent deeds. The avid taste of the savages for liquor was supplied, in general, by carefully doled-out portions from the general store-room of the fort, as highly-prized gifts;

45. *Johnson Mss.*, 15, 90.
46. *Memorial to Dartmouth, Dartmouth Mss.*, February 10th, 1773.

but smugglers were constantly attempting to evade Johnson's strict embargo upon the sale of alcohol, for it was the most profitable medium of exchange; he wrote to Johnson:

Every hour my uneasiness is increased. In spite of my vigilance, I fear we will have mischief done.[47]

The arduousness of his labours began to tell upon him. He was obliged to employ clerks constantly, recording every minute instance of charity or generosity to the begging savages, and reporting it to every other northern commissary; to preserve, besides the strictest accounts, a journal of all Indian intelligences; to keep in constant touch with the east, and to make long journeys into the Indian land. He could not attempt to impose Johnson's restrictions upon trade, for the ministry had made, through the influence of Sir Guy Carleton, the governor of Canada, an exception for the trade north of Mackinac; but he required every trader who went wintering among the Indians to give a bond for his good behaviour, and another in guarantee that he would return his furs through the post, and not carry them down the Mississippi to New Orleans.

In July and August he thus licensed one hundred and twenty canoes of goods, paddled by traders from the fort into Lakes Huron, Superior or Michigan. Each trader was required to bring back observations on the numbers and temper of the Indians he dealt with. At the same time, Roberts was kept busy issuing clothing and food to needy braves, giving presents to groups of influential individuals, and receiving with affable kindness deputations of chiefs. His task, weighing his meagre resources, had been rendered doubly difficult by Rogers' excessive generosity, but his tact and sense stood him in good stead. He was able to report to his superior:

The Indians complain Rogers promises more than he can perform, and say he has more love for packs, but less sense, than me.[48]

---

47. *Johnson Mss.*; 13, 134.
48. *Johnson Mss.*, 15, 90.

Long afterwards he declared:

Though no Englishman dared trade far down Lake Michigan, all the Indians thereabouts sent me invitations to visit them, and paid me a great compliment by saying they would look upon me as one of themselves.[49]

His knowledge of their language, his kindly cordiality, even his volatility, where it inflamed him into a desire to protect them, rapidly won him their warm regard.

But he and Rogers continued more and more jealous, suspicious, and sullen in their attitude toward one another. Rogers' debts, joined with the news that his heavy drafts were meeting with protests in New York, and would likely be returned to him, was driving him into increasing moodiness and discontent. He grew troubled, quarrelsome, and irritable. In July Potter returned from his trip upon Lake Superior, and three or four days later the entire garrison was amazed to see the door of Rogers' house fly violently open, and the two emerge, scuffling, fighting, and blaspheming one another, down the steps. They separated after a moment, and strode away from each other, white and panting, but without divulging the root of the sudden and amazing quarrel. The soldiery were agog, and watched the two men closely. On the morrow they indulged in high words on the parade ground, and on the third day, meeting again, Rogers flew into a violent passion, knocked Potter down, and ordered him put in irons.

On the advice of Roberts and others, however, Potter applied to Spiessmacher for protection, and received it. He nevertheless still declined to make any statement as to the cause of this altercation with one so long his protector and friend, and it was generally supposed that the affair was the mere outgrowth of Rogers' violent frame of mind. The soldiers in especial remained almost unanimously loyal to the governor. Roberts, abetted more and more by Spiessmacher, inclined to put the worst possible construction upon his acts.[50]

---

49. *Memorial to Dartmouth,* February 10th, 1773.

50. For this, and references also for matter in the (continued on next page)

The sharp final explosion between the two men was not long delayed. During the early days of August it seemed clear to Roberts that Rogers, in desperation, was putting some huge and nefarious scheme under way. Atherton and Tute he had sent out down Lake Michigan, on some unknown mission; he himself was constantly engaged in receiving belts and making speeches, of which he would let Roberts know nothing; Stuart and his other agents about the fort were suspiciously busy. The whisper began to go throughout the settlement that the governor intended in the spring to gather his associates about him, sack the place, and proceed southward by way of La Baye, Lake Michigan, and the Illinois river to join the French and Spanish beyond the Mississippi. The various merchants and traders to whom Rogers was in debt—and he was said to owe several hundred thousand French *livres*—and who held large stocks of seizable goods, came to Roberts in great alarm, with such fervent prayers that he protect them and their property that he made a secret agreement with Spiessmacher to cut short any attempted evasion of the governor. The secretary, Potter, still sulking and silent, was making dilatory plans to leave the fort and go to England. He hinted at times to Robert's of matters of weighty importance which he might disclose, and which, he said, his conscience strongly urged him to lay before Johnson, in full written form. As the middle of the month passed, the commissary reported to his chief at Albany that it had become an open secret that Rogers had declared, unless some ray of hope were offered him in his present gloomy circumstances, he would "go off in the spring, and not empty-handed." Stephen Groesbeck, one of the richest

succeeding pages not otherwise ascribed, see *New York Colonial Documents*, VII, 988, 990, 993. and 997; *Documentary History of New York*, II, 883, 885, 888, 895; *Canadian Archives*, Series Q, Volume 4, 304-307, Series Q, Volume 5, part 2, 607-611; *Johnson Mss.*, 16: 123, 134, 144; 17: 4, 13, 154, etc ; Dr. F. B. Hough's edition of *Rogers' Journals*, Albany, 1850, Appendix; Wisconsin *Historical Collections*, XII, 27-37; *Michigan Pioneer and Historical Collections*, X, 224-233. As most of these references deal with the events of one or two days, to state the varied authorities for each single fact would involve useless repetition. In this account it should be kept in mind that although all Rogers' contemporaries recognized that there were two sides to the whole affair, we have no means of stating in full just what the major's case was; for only the accusations of his enemies have been preserved.

merchants at the post, whom Roberts characterized as "a heavy, self-interested Dutchman," was the governor's creditor for several thousand pounds, covered only by worthless drafts upon the Indian department He seemed deeply interested in Rogers' machinations, and had sent out a messenger with belts to the Indians of the north-west. Roberts wrote:

> Rogers says that if affairs to the north-west don't turn out luckily, he must go off, and it's thought Groesbeck won t stay behind.

It was known, too, that the commander had been instrumental in sending eleven canoes loaded with goods to Lake Superior, and was now anxiously awaiting their return.

Finally, on the night of August 19th, Roberts was awakened about midnight by the noise of some traders carrying rum from the fort's storehouse down to the water. He refrained from interfering at the time, but as soon as it grew light began an investigation. From some source he secured certain evidence that the smuggling of rum out of the fort had reached a great magnitude within the last few days, and that a number of kegs had been landed, with Rogers' full knowledge and approbation, at a small island on the way to La Baye, where they were to be used in gaining political and commercial credit with the Indians.

In great excitement he called in Potter, and summoned him to give all the information he possessed of the governor's plots. After some hesitation, assumed or real, the ex-secretary unfolded his entire story. He said that Rogers had determined a full month before, that, if his plan for the civil government of Mackinac did not elicit a favourable reply from England during the ensuing winter, he would close at once with an offer he had received from the French through one of his old comrades in the provincial service, Captain Hopkins, now a turncoat in the West Indies.[51] With Tute, Goddard, Atherton, and whatever part

51. "Captain Hopkins," wrote Johnson to Shelburne, "of Maryland, formerly of the 18th Regiment, obtained a captain's commission in the Queen s Independents, on the reduction of which he entered the French service, and is now (1767) a colonel in Hispaniola. A great intimacy always subsisted between him and Rogers." An alleged letter of his to Rogers, exhorting the latter to (continued on next page)

of the garrison he could induce to desert, Potter' further alleged, he planned to rifle all the trading depots in the vicinity, and thus "full-handed" join the French west of the Illinois country.[52]

It was his own refusal to adhere to this plan, said Potter, which had occasioned his quarrel with Rogers, who had threatened him with instant death if he revealed it. Trembling with indignation, Roberts at once sat down and penned a decisive note to Spiessmacher, impeaching "Robert Rogers, Esquire, for holding secret correspondence with the enemies of Great Britain, and forming conspiracies," and exhorting the captain to "seize his person and papers, among which you will find sufficient proof." This he sealed, directed, and sent at once by a messenger. He then wrote a full letter to Johnson; and a third to Daniel Claus, introducing Potter, and desiring that he be allowed to repeat his accusation in Montreal under oath. These two he gave to Potter to transmit.

By this time the fire of his wrath was somewhat abated, and he was able to hold himself under restraint. He called his clerk, John Hanson, and, going out upon the parade ground, applied to Rogers for a sergeant and two men to send with Hanson to seize the contraband rum.[53] A proof of the bad feeling existing between the men lies in the fact that before he reluctantly acquiesced in their going, the major forced the commissary to promise to pay the soldiers for their time.

They were absent some hours, and in the interim Roberts halted seven canoes which had reached the fort, forbidding them to proceed into a region where, for aught they knew, all the savages might be maddened and blood-thirsty with liquor.

---

join the French, and speaking of disgraces which Rogers had endured, was later found among the major's effects, and is given in *New York Colonial Documents*, VII, 993.

52. Louisiana was at this time properly Spanish; but the French still held many offices of more than local control. Cf. *P. R. O., C. O. 5,* 86; Gage to Hillsborough, October, 1768: "There is such a strange mixture of French and Spanish government on the opposite side of the Mississippi that there is no knowing to whom the country belongs. A French officer, M. St. Ange, commands on the Mississippi, and receives orders from both Don Ulloa and M. Aubry."

53. Some time previously Roberts had quarrelled with Hanson, and had cautioned Johnson to receive no information through him. See *Johnson Mss.,* 15, 125.

At the end of the period the two boats he had dispatched grated heavily on the pebbly beach, and Hanson supervised the rolling out of several kegs of rum over the gunwale of each. As "seizing-officer," Roberts felt the disposition of the rum to be his, and ordered it to be placed in the king's store, of which he held the key; but Rogers, who was standing by, glowering, sharply contradicted his directions, commanding that it be given to the deputy commissary of provisions. A heated quarrel ensued, in which both the excitable commissary, highly wrought upon by all he had heard, and the imperious governor lost their heads; the lie was exchanged; a denunciation as traitor trembled on the lips of Roberts; and Rogers in a rage called the guard, and had the struggling officer, before the amazed eyes of the Indians and townspeople, borne away and locked up in his house.

Affairs had now gone so far that interference from the east was inevitable. At Mackinac, however, it seemed for a time that the direct quarrel between the two officers might be glossed over. Roberts was not long kept in durance, for on August 22nd, after testifying with others at a court of inquiry into the seizure of rum, over which Rogers presided, he was released. A temporary reconciliation followed, but one merely temporary; for Roberts' knowledge of Rogers' secret designs made it impossible for him to avoid a. renewal of the disputes.

Early in September he was again under arrest, and by September 21st felt his confinement so deeply that he addressed to Spiessmacher a petition praying for relief.[54] Finally he grew wholly insubordinate, denouncing Rogers as a traitor on every hand, and was sent eastward in irons, to await trial under General Gage.

Meanwhile, on August 29th, Potter had set out for Montreal, and a month later made deposition there under oath as to all of Rogers' plots, sailing immediately thereafter to England. This deposition, together with Roberts' letter, reached Gage and Johnson in October, and produced a real sensation. Johnson writes:

---

54. *Johnson Mss.*, 15: 44, 55.

From Potter's character I have no doubt he will make the most of his discoveries; at the same time, I believe his account is within compass.

Already, on September 15th, upon hearing of his enormous expenditures, Gage had decided to remove Rogers. Now a new order was sent to Spiessmacher, directing him to arrest the major, and confine him until he might be brought to Montreal to trial; and to seize all his property, especially any goods with which he had been trading, to satisfy his creditors.[55]

On December 6th Roberts arrived at New York, with more than twenty affidavits from Mackinac of his own unfitness and misconduct, to report to Gage for trial; and on the same day Rogers was arrested at the far western post by Spiessmacher, on a charge of high treason.[56]

Throughout the winter Rogers remained confined to his house, closely watched by Spiessmacher and Lieutenant Christie, now second in command. From the first these gentlemen reported that they found something very suspicious in his behaviour. For his own part, he complained that he was loaded with irons, kept in a fireless room, open to the full inclemency of the freezing weather, and scarcely allowed the necessities of

---

55. "Major Rogers has goods trading for his benefit in the Indian country to a very considerable amount, and the returns may soon be in, as I am informed." *Documentary History of New York*, II, 888.

56. Gage wrote on this date to Johnson: "Which of the two men is most in fault I can't say; most probably both of them in some degree." On October 9th Sir Guy Carleton, writing to the Earl of Shelburne in regard to the matter, said of the root of the difficulty: "From the fact that a jealousy about presents, which certainly amounts to no inconsiderable sum, it being the constant custom of both traders and Indians to present some at their arrival and departure from these posts, and which, from being the usual perquisite of the commandant, are now become the commissary's, occasions disputes and misrepresentations constantly on both sides, I submit that all presents of value, from either Indians or traders, should be absolutely declined by the officers of the crown. . . . It must be acknowledged that Mr. Potter bears but a very bad character. . . . and may be actuated by views of self-interest and motives of revenge; unhappy it is for Major Rogers that his character does not stand in so fair a light as to permit a neglect of Potter's information; the less so that the distresses resulting from his extravagance may give weight to a suspicion of his using some extraordinary means to extricate himself." Potter, by reason of his ill-health, was not expected to reach Europe. *Canadian Archives*, Series 4, Volume 4, 304-7.

life He was robbed also of his effects, "to the. value of several thousand pounds, of his papers, and of the maps he had taken, at great expense, of the Indians' country;" while his wife "was treated with the same inhumanity as himself, and exposed to the insults of the common soldiers."[57]

Under these circumstances, and in collusion with his orderly, David Fullerton, he laid plans to escape, first approaching a Canadian, Joseph Ans.[58] Rogers' alleged plot was to have the savages decoy Spiessmacher and Christie out of the fort, when—as most of the soldiers were yet his fast friends——he could seize the keys, sack Mackinac and Detroit, and march away to the Illinois. Ans betrayed the attempt to Spiessmacher, first taking him to a point where he could hear one of their conferences, and later securing from Rogers a promissory note for £500 if Ans would carry him safely to a force commanded by Captain Hopkins on the Mississippi.[59] As a result of this exposure the major's orderly was arrested, and the guard about his house, previously relaxed, was resumed.

In the spring the sloop expected for Rogers' conveyance arrived, and he was put on board to be transported to Niagara.[60] He afterwards testified:

---

57. Memorial to Hillsborough, December 21st, 1768. *P. R. O., C. O. 5,* Volume 70, 235.

58. Joseph Louis Ans (or Ainse) was born at Mackinac, May 1st, 1744. Soon after his information against Rogers he was taken into English employ as an interpreter. In 1790 he was convicted of having embezzled government stores for his own trading ventures. *Michigan Pioneer and Historical Collections,* XI, 491.

59. "The French had two battalions waiting for him," Ans reported Rogers as saying, "under Colonel Hopkins, who had often written to him." Spiessmacher testified that the major's orderly broke down and confessed the plot when taxed with it, and that Rogers had had Ans brought up from St. Joseph in the spring of 1767, ostensibly as an interpreter, but really to use him as a messenger between himself and Hopkins, to invite Hopkins to come with a few men and receive possession of the fort.

60. Navigation in the straits became possible about May 1st. See *P. R. O., C. O. 5,* 86; Gage to Hillsborough, August 17, 1768. "Some disturbance happened at Mackinac, on the occasion of sending Major Rogers from that fort to Detroit; a disorderly tribe of the Chippewa went there with their arms, and threw their English belts into the lake, and invited other nations to join them to release the major from his confinement. The officer commanding tried to satisfy them by various methods, but at length put the garrison under arms, and with two armed boats put him on board the vessel."

I was thrown into the hold of the vessel, upon the ballast of stones, still in irons; and in this manner, transported the whole distance. When they were taken off, the weight of them was so considerable, and they were fastened so tightly, that my legs were bent. From the pain I suffered, together with the cold, the bone of my right leg was split, and the marrow forced its way out of it through the skin.[61]

At Niagara he received the charges against him from General Gage, and was taken on, under strong guard, to be tried at Montreal. Almost immediately upon his arrival there it was decided to alter the charge against him from treason to mutiny.[62] In the first place, it was desired that he be brought before an official of the bar at once, without the delays and useless formality of a civil trial; and high treason was a crime under the cognizance of the civil, mutiny under the military law. For his part, Rogers was anxious to prolong his trial upon several pretences, chief of which was that he required time to bring his witnesses up from Mackinac.

As a second consideration, it was at once perceived by his prosecutors that there was a failure of sufficient evidence to convict him of really treasonable conduct. Potter had gone to England for his health, and Chief-Justice Hay pronounced that in common law the affidavit made out by him, as coming from a man of doubtful character, and one who had just quarrelled violently with Rogers, could do no material injury to the latter. One of the chief pieces of evidence for the state, an alleged letter of Hopkins', found among Rogers' effects, which urged him to make haste to join with the French, Rogers declared to be an arrant forgery. It had been transmitted to him, immediately upon leaving for the west, by Johnson, and, dated San Domingo, April 9th, 1766, was signed "Maryland"

"I always thought, and am still of the opinion," said the major, "that it was penned on the Mohawk River. I returned it to General Gage, but by some magic art my letters miscarried."[63]

61. *Memorial to Hillsborough*, December 21st, 1768. *P. R. O., C. O. 5*, Volume 70, 235.
62. *Johnson Mss.*, 16: 123, 134, 144.
63. *P. R. O., C. O. 5*, Volume 70, 235.

Of other tangible evidence of so serious a crime, except the rumours upon which Roberts and Spiessmacher had based their suspicions, there was very little. Yet Rogers had wrought too much evil to go unprosecuted. With the new charge of mutinous conduct were joined accusations of disobedience to Gage and Johnson, and of embezzlement of goods and funds to his own purpose at the fort, and preparations were made to have the requisite witnesses at the fort relieved from duty and sent down, from Mackinac at once.[64] Claus wrote to Johnson:

In his grinning way Rogers makes a light matter of his crime, and tells the merchants that if they supported him he would soon return to his post.

This support was no more than a fair exchange, for these were the persons Rogers had endeavoured to aid in his policy with regard to the Indian trade; and as he was greatly their debtor, it was obviously to their interest that they should clear him. Rogers friend Goddard was charged with assisting him in his second crime—the embezzlement of money and goods. There was a general inclination to let him off easily, however, as his influence with the Indians, manifested in a number of ways, had shown in him the possibility of a most useful public servant. Tute, Atherton, and the others were out of reach, and no particular effort was made to secure them. Not until early October did the trial, delayed by the necessity of bringing witnesses of the prosecution, and by Rogers' own indisposition from disease brought on by his excesses and dissipations, begin.

There was some difficulty in obtaining the testimony of Roberts, who had been almost as deeply involved as Rogers himself in debt, suits, and legal difficulties ever since he had been sent home a prisoner from Mackinac, and who, while awaiting the opening of the trial in Montreal, was shortly arrested at the instance of one Morrison of Oswego, with whom he had disputed regarding the trade during his commissaryship there.

For the defence Rogers had a number of witnesses, and all his accounts, certified to by some of his officers as proper and

64. *Johnson Mss.*, 16, 123.

necessary, besides other documents. Against him Spiessmacher, Christie, and others testified, and Potter's affidavit and Hopkins' letter were adduced; but the case utterly collapsed through want of more confirmatory evidence. Johnson explained:

> The gentlemen concerned in the prosecution did not have the same desire to do him a prejudice as himself and sundry others had to manifest his innocence, and induce the public to deem the whole a malicious attack upon a man of worth.

Of the details of the trial no record has been preserved.

During the closing days of the hearing, while still ignorant of how it was tending, Rogers addressed a memorial to Hillsborough from prison.

> I make not the least doubt that I am honourably acquitted, although witnesses were hired to swear falsely against me, and my most material ones prevented from coming down.

After a detailed account of the cruelty of his treatment he continues:

> My being cleared alone is not sufficient; I must have an opportunity of clearing up my character, for which purpose I beg an order that Mr. Roberts, Captain Spiessmacher, and Lieutenant Christie may be confined and court-martialled; and that I may go up country to bring down my proper evidence, and few remaining effects.

He asked also for a new appointment, either in America or the East Indies, and stated that he intended coming to England in the autumn. He made it evident at the same time, by some insulting inquiries which he addressed to Gage regarding that officer's failure to prosecute Roberts, that his temper was dangerous. And so, in December, the trial broke up. Johnson wrote to Gage:

> I hope that any affairs of party arising from the proceedings may totally subside. If not, it will be easy to see what keeps it up.

Such a subsidence, as the event proved, was out of the question; and Rogers' resentment, carried before his powerful friends in England, was to be the force to keep it up. The major, nursing his anger at what Johnson himself called the "indignities" he had received, remained in Montreal during the winter limping sadly on his injured leg, and everywhere commiserated.

Early in May he had a vicious quarrel with Roberts in the public streets of the city, and, asking him "if he would give him satisfaction for bribing Potter to swear his life away," halted him with his cane before an excited crowd of townspeople, called him puppy, tweaked his nose, and challenged him to a duel.

The military commander in the city was forced to put both men under a bond to keep the peace; but Roberts nevertheless complained that "Jones won't believe Rogers carries arms, and all that is said by everybody seems prepossessed in his favour."[65]

Already the major was skilfully trying, with success in Montreal at least, to turn the tables of public sentiment upon his enemies. At the coming of summer he took ship for England.

---

65. *Johnson Mss.*, 17, 154.

CHAPTER 5

The American Revolution

There was a multiplicity of motives to lure Rogers upon his second journey to England. His most powerful friends were there, as his most powerful enemies were in America. His financial affairs at home lay in utter ruin, and by the expedient of a quick passage he might escape his debtors until they could instruct London agents to continue harrying him. To the public he was still favourably known across the water; while in his own country, although he had his eager partisans in Canada, where many were induced to believe that he had been spitefully wronged by the tools of Johnson, a general ill-savour attached to his name. Finally, his angry resentment against the commander-in-chief and the superintendent of Indian affairs made it a daily humiliation to remain longer upon a continent in which they were in power.

His three direct purposes at the seat of empire were to work some malice against the party of Johnson; to obtain a fresh appointment in some part of King George's wide dominions; and somehow, by obtaining payment for his losses at Mackinac and elsewhere, to find his way through all the mazes of his indebtedness to solvency. His liabilities totalled thirteen thousand pounds, and to keep himself from falling into a debtor's prison was his immediate care.

In May, soon after his street-quarrel with Roberts, he had left Montreal and proceeded to New York, closely dogged by his creditors, where he importuned Gage for his pay as commandant at Mackinac. The general refused him, upon the ground that as his appointment was made by the London minister, it could not go in the American accounts; an answer which filled the shrewd major with mingled regret and rejoicing, as it led him to believe that he had never lost his commission, and was still on the active payroll.[1] He was able, however, to secure immediate payment of his expenses at Montreal, and upon these slender resources, having secured signed leave of absence, he left for the mother country in June.[2]

At his arrival in the capital he went into residence near the old house of the Penn family, at Spring Gardens and Charing Cross, a very busy and somewhat fashionable part of London. Here he renewed his acquaintance with William Fitzherbert and other of his old military and political friends in the city, and set himself to use every possible patron.

During October he reopened the communication which he had begun with Hillsborough while in prison, narrating in full the grievances and injuries he had suffered since his appointment, and asking that his lordship lend his potent influence to have him remunerated for his labours in the north-west. He waited, too, upon Hillsborough at that officer's public levees, with such allies as he could induce thus personally to push his suit;[3] and simultaneously sent in a detailed account of his arrears of pay to the Treasury.[4]

Certificates of his usefulness and bravery he secured from almost every considerable American leader during the Seven Years War, Amherst, Abercrombie, Howe, Moncton, Webb, Loudoun, Eglinton, and others; some of them, delivered with an alacrity strongly suggestive of jealousy of Gage and Johnson, added warm personal recommendations to the more perfunctory testimonials.[5]

He became once more a familiar figure at parties and public receptions. Finally, as a crowning mark of distinction, Fitzher-

1. *P. R. O., C. O. 5*, Volume 70, 699.
2. *Johnson Mss.*, 18, 185.
3. *P. R. O., C. O. 5*, Volume 70, 691-9.
4. *Idem*, p. 627.
5. *Johnson Mss.*, 19, 112.

bert presented him to George III, whose royal hand he kissed and to whom he offered in person a petition for the reissuance of the lands once given him on Lake Champlain.[6] So visibly powerful were his friends, whether disinterested patrons or the enemies of Johnson, that for the moment he became presumptuous in his requests. A correspondent of Johnson's reported in February 1770:

> The minister (Hillsborough) asked what would content him, he desired to be made a baronet, with a pension of 600 sterling, to be restored to his governorship at Mackinac, and to have all his account paid.[7]

Although these requests were beyond reason, the fruits of his energetic contrivances and motions were soon apparent.

In January, 1770, he presented a final petition to Hillsborough, emphasizing the fact that he was an innocent, injured man, cleared of the unjust aspersions thrown upon him, and reiterating his desire to return to his post whenever he had been enabled to meet his obligations.[8] The secretary of state was at some pains to lay the matter before the Treasury Board in proper form, and within a few days Grey Cooper, its secretary, informed Rogers that he should be paid as commandant at Mackinac to December 21st, 1769, a date chosen as terminating four years of service under the commission of 1765.[9]

Good fortune came not singly. With his arrears in salary were also paid his accounts for Carver's expedition to the west, covering bills not merely for the supplies with which he had outfitted his subordinate in 1766, but for those, more meagre in quantity, which he had attempted to forward the lieutenant early the next year at the Falls of St. Anthony.[10] He was assisted in this by Carver himself, a fresh arrival in England, who had petitioned successfully during the summer for the eight-

---

6. *Idem*, 18, 185. *P. R. O.*, *C. O. 5*, Volume 1074, 385–
7. William Rivington; *Johnson Mss.*, 18, 185.
8. *P. R. O.*, *C. O. 5*, Volume 70, 701.
9. *Treasury Minutes*, December 21st, 1769; July 13, 1770.
10. *Johnson Mss.*, 18, 185.

shilling wage which Rogers had offered him.[11] There was thus appropriated to the major at the beginning of 1770 more than £3000—a truly rejuvenating relief, enabling him to throw several sops to his pack of creditors, and to secure a new hold upon means of subsistence in the city. He continued, however, to pray for his salary as Indian commissioner at Mackinac, for his collateral expenses, and for the goods he had given as presents to the Indians—an enormous sum still. At the same time, having definitely lost his post, he began to push his claims upon the government for a new situation in India or America.

In his political objects, Rogers met for a time with success. Roberts had sailed for London in March, 1770, with letters of recommendation from Johnson Hall, and with several diplomatic and business commissions to execute for the Indian department. Like Rogers, he was so head over heels in debt that he could escape from his creditors only with difficulty, and before taking ship was forced to secure a transfer of suit in an embarrassing damage case brought by the Mackinac merchants whose rum he had confiscated;[12] and he, too, hoped to mend his fortunes by securing payment of £1000 which he had expended in the king's service.[13]

Long before he sailed. he received reports that "Rogers was making a noise in England," and implored Johnson to secure protectors for him against one who "might keep me in hot water."[14] When shown on the eve of his departure "the extra-. ordinary letter from London which told of Rogers court presentation, he wrote again to his superior:

I suppose I shall find a strong party against me by Rogers, and wish you might send something to the ministry that would be useful to support me against the clamour. It would be disgraceful to see that scoundrel honoured, and I that have served thirteen years unblemished unnoticed.[15]

---

11. Carver had testified that it was "in consequence of Rogers commission that he undertook and performed his great journey." *Board of Trade, Commercial Papers,*Volume 459.
12. *Johnson Mss.*, 19, 163.
13. Petitions of May 27th and June 9th, 1773, Earl of Dartmouth's unpublished papers.
14. *Johnson Mss.*, 19, 179.
15. *Idem*, 19, 185.

From the unusual care with which Johnson equipped his agent, it was clear that he also had a regard for the pertinacity and vigour with which the ex-commandant was organizing all the existing opposition to the American regime. Nor were their forebodings amiss. Roberts had immediate difficulty in seeing Hillsborough, before whom he was to lay a plea that the Northern Department be allowed more funds, and only after repeated visits did he "make his lordship recollect that Johnson had mentioned him in letters."[16] A similar coldness elsewhere convinced him that every-where his paths had been poisoned, and his character defamed, by his wily enemy. Early in August, after a month of fruitless endeavours, he reported:

Rogers story is much attended to by those of the great, who are only too glad to censure any reputation better than their own. Until that fellow is sent somewhere, I shall be continually plagued with contradicting his vile story.[17]

He had lost his position by his trip to England, and even this fact the major used against him, his second letter complains:

Rogers has reported that I was turned out of employment for the ill-treatment I gave him, and he has been too much believed. It is unfortunate that I can't be introduced to more men in authority, and so contradict in person what I am obliged to do through various channels.[18]

Finally, the widespread nature of the dislike which he found had been inspired for Johnson and his colleague plainly puzzled him. He tactfully informed his own immediate chief:

It is a little odd how Rogers has procured aid from Amherst, Abercrombie, and almost every other field officer. It seems a party against General Gage, but time will clear it up, and honesty triumph.[19]

It was, however, only so long as Rogers was able to give

---

16. *Idem*, 19, 112.
17. *Idem*, 19, 172.
18. June 12, 1770. *Johnson Mss.*, 19, 112.
19. *Idem*, 19, 112.

head to a temporary sentiment against the American officers that his affairs prospered; and when the small furore to which his charges, his loud complaints, and his bitter vapourings gave rise had subsided, and the novelty of his petty attacks had spent itself in vain, he was once more relegated to the chilly ante-rooms of noblemen, and spent his time in the composition of unavailing petitions for further relief. Fitzherbert, it is true, remained for some time longer his faithful friend, so that Roberts was informed in October, 1770, that three of the ministry intended providing for Rogers, and that it was thought he would get a post in the East India service.[20] At the same time, the major found ready allies in his creditors, anxious to help him, through their London agents, to the money which would satisfy their own demands. Six different firms, with extensive business and political connections, were all, in Roberts expressive phrase, "pushing for him" during the period that he seemed basking in official favour. But they were ready to turn upon him the moment his affairs took a darker turn—a moment which, so far was he out of his depth financially, so beyond reason were most of the claims in his total of £10,000, even his energy and assurance could no longer postpone. As summer passed he who had once "hummed all the great people"[21] had gained nothing. In May, 1771, he had fruitlessly petitioned the Board of Trade for his huge grant on Lake Champlain, which, he said, "he meant to occupy and cultivate."[22] For the Board's refusal he had had in part to thank his old rival, for a few days previously, at Hillsborough's instance, Roberts "was examined before the Board, and given an opportunity to make known the treatment he received from Rogers, and to show them how far they had been imposed upon."[23]

Other memorials met a like fate, and matters went rapidly from bad to worse. In November, 1771, he made a personal appeal to Hillsborough in terms that have a note of desperation in them.

20. *Idem*, 19, 112, 226.
21. *Johnson Mss.*, 18, 186.
22. *P. R. O., C. O. 5*, Volume 1075, 117.
23. *Johnson Mss.*, 20, 230.

No man, my lord, has gone through more vicissitudes of alternate hardship and success than myself and I urge my case with greater confidence, now that prejudice has had time to subside, and the world is disposed to be just to my character.

The hackneyed story of his long services and unjust persecution follows; and he concludes:

I was without cause dismissed from employ, and do now stand consigned to inanity, and almost absolute want, with an enormous responsibility to my expenditures on credit in the ranging and Indian services. I implore your lordship to consider and commiserate my situation.

Yet he asked only for a renewal of his commission as major, with pay of fifteen shillings daily.[24] In February, 1772, he prayed the Treasury to find means for presenting his demands to the House of Commons—a request utterly and absurdly impracticable.[25]

Reports home of his activities thenceforth became meagre, for he was no longer a person of sufficient importance to figure in the letters to New York from London. Despite his many discouragements, he continued to petition for his pay as commissary to Mackinac, and, on August 10, 1772 wrote a curt note to Sir William Johnson for a certificate of his appointment "to manage Indian affairs at Mackinac, as also for a statement of the commissary's usual allowance."[26] At length his debtors passed from urgency to threats, and from threats to action.

Early in March, 1773, one of them, Robert Hunter, had lost patience, and unsuccessfully petitioned the treasury for the value of the merchandise supplied the major in the north-west in 1767.[27] The pack to whom he owed money immediately closed in. On June 14, he was in the Fleet Prison for debt, complaining bitterly that he was in distress for want of every necessity, and

24. *P. R. O., C. O. 5,* Volume 154, 18.
25. *Treasury Minutes,* February, 1772.
26. *Johnson Mss.,* 21, 238.
27. *Treasury Minutes,* March 7, 1773.

greatly injured in his health by his long and close confinement.[28] In a neighbouring cell was Benjamin Roberts, who, having drawn on Johnson for £100 to maintain himself in England, had been summarily deserted by his old friend and patron.

One of the last straws at which Rogers clutched was a reopening of his old proposal for a search after the Northwest Passage in a plan presented to the Privy Council in February, 1772. As he had done seven years before, he set before the council his unusual qualifications for such a search, stating that as a commander at the Great Lake posts, and in "various expeditions which he has made or caused to be made therefrom," he "has gained information which almost positively established the existence of a navigable passage"; and he prayed "to be employed in this time of peace in such an expedition, at a salary of £3 per day as director and conductor of the enterprise. He estimated that in all the trip would consume three years, and although he insisted upon a party of sixty, including several officers, a geographer, cartographers, pioneers, and fifty hunters, he believed that £17 10s daily would suffice for salaries. The itinerary of his earlier proposal he changed but slightly. Leaving from the Mohawk in April or May, he would traverse the Great Lakes and Wisconsin to the Falls of St. Anthony, and there pass the first winter; the second summer he would push on to the Pacific, where he would again halt; and at the coming of the third spring, he would strike north and north-east along the coast, following its rounding contour, and exploring every considerable inlet, until he found the one which really connected the Atlantic with the Pacific. In its return the party would pass through Japan, Siberia, and Russia. The plan never received really serious consideration, although it was transmitted from the Privy Council to a committee, thence to the Board of Trade, and finally to the Treasury.[29]

Of Rogers' movements between the middle of June, 1773, and the middle of March, 1775, we know almost nothing. On the former date, he petitioned to the king from Fleet Prison to grant him "sixty miles square on the banks of some great and

28. *Acts of the Privy Council,* VI. 538. Colonial Series, unpublished paper.
29. P. R. O., C. O. *323,* Volume 27, 143.

convenient river or lake in America, that he might compromise with his creditors." Although his memorial was recommended by six of these unwearied pursuers, and by thirteen general officers who had at some time served in America, including many names of distinction, it was refused.[30]

The blank of twenty months which follows was one of importance to an officer connected with both English and American affairs, for it was a period which saw the two peoples rapidly uniting into war. The silence broken finally by a petition from Rogers to the Earl of Dartmouth, Hillsborough's successor as secretary of state for America, announcing the major's intention of rejoining the army, and asking for a renewal of his commission, as "it will prove of infinite service to him in many respects." He had at that date evidently been contemplating for some time re-entrance into active service; for he mentions that he had left his commission at one of the under-secretaries desk several weeks before, and that he had repeatedly applied for the renewal to Lord Barrington, "who had absolutely refused to do any services for him.[31]

But how had he escaped the debtors cell? And how had he spent the last twelvemonth? As to the first of these questions, we know only that his brother James, already a rich land holder in New York, had assumed by bond his most pressing obligations;[32] not, however, before Rogers was in such desperate straits that he had attempted a legal prosecution of Gage to reimburse himself for his expenditures in the north-west—a step which the ministry hastily stopped. As to the second, we have only Rogers' unverified statement of a later date to President Wheelock of Dartmouth College, that he had fought two battles under the Bey of Algiers.[33]

At all events, early in 1775 he was still in London, free from his most immediate difficulties, interested in the threatening aspect of colonial affairs, and anxious to see service again, either in

30. Acts of the Privy Council, VI, 538.
31. *Dartmouth Mss.*, Petition of March 13, 1775.
32. *American Archives*, Series 4, Volume 3, 865-8.
33. *American Archives*, Series 4, Volume 3, 265.

America or in India. For a time it seemed probable that he would go to the latter held, for Dartmouth not only restored him to his majority, upon half-pay, but recommended an application which he made to the directors of the East India Company; parliament resolved during the spring, however, to send no additional officers there, and his reviving hopes fell short of their mark.

He at once turned to the other alternative, and, representing to Harrington that he was seized with a burning desire to visit his family in the New World, and that business affairs required his immediate presence there, sailed on June 4, 1775, from Gravesend.[34]

Before leaving England he was advised by his political friends that if he wished to obtain service in America he would do well to attempt a repair of his breach with Gage, widened so far by his loud speeches in London in 1769-70, and by his more recent steps in law.[35] Immediately upon arriving in September at Baltimore, therefore, he wrote the commander-in-chief expressing "equal hope and firm desire that every past unhappy circumstance should be buried in oblivion." It was clear that as soon as he had completed matters of business in the rebellious provinces, he hoped again to receive a command under the British flag. Meanwhile, as he halted a few days in Baltimore to acquaint himself with the revolutionized posture of affairs in Spanish America, he assumed a wisely conciliatory and cordial attitude toward his revolted countrymen.

Lexington and Bunker Hill were now months-old stories; Boston was invested, and Washington had just assumed command of the besiegers; Rogers' old comrade, Israel Putnam, had been chosen one of the four major-generals of the colonial army; and the Continental Congress was sitting at Philadelphia, where a few days since it had simultaneously set forth the necessity of taking up arms and owned the continuing sovereignty of the king. Rogers was filled with shocked amazement at the new spirit of resistance abroad among the colonists, writing to the home government that—

---

34. *Idem,*Volume 4, 158.

35. *Dartmouth Mss.*, Rogers to Pownall, October 3, 1775.

. . . . since my arrival here I have done all I can to un-deceive these people, now labouring under an unhappy delusion.[36]

However, he found it necessary to wait on the Continental Congress at Philadelphia, on September 22nd, to obtain a permit to close his debts in lower New York, and to arrange his affairs with his brother, resident above Albany. He was duly given this passport, over Franklin's signature, upon a promise neither to bear arms against the colonies, nor to supply information concerning their defences to Gage or to the ministry.[37] While in Philadelphia, nevertheless, he did not conceal the fact that he was on half pay, and considered himself yet a loyal officer in the king's army, and his attitude here toward the American radicals seems to have been one of rather unfriendly neutrality. Nor did he hesitate, upon reaching New York, to open negotiations with both Gage and Dartmouth for a command, complaining of the impossibility of maintaining himself and his family upon half-pay. In the city he lodged at "Dr. Harrison's on Broadway," and was under the surveillance of the local committee of safety during every moment of his stay. In fact, he seems never to have entertained, nor to have given others the impression of entertaining, any disposition to adhere to the cause of his fellow provincials.[38]

While his military future was still unsettled, he devoted himself to business. From Governor Tryon he secured a reissue of several old grants of land along the New Hampshire boundary line, with which to satisfy his creditors;[39] and early in October he set out north through Albany, to join his family, and to visit his various friends and relatives. He was halted on the road by what he called "a severe attack of fever and ague," but finally pushed on to his brother James in Kent, near the Connecticut. He then proceeded to Portsmouth, where he stayed a few days with his wife and young son, at the home of his aged and

36. *Dartmouth Mss.*, Rogers to Pownall, October 3, 1775.
37. *American Archives*, Series 4, Volume 3, 865-8.
38. *American Archives,* Series 4, Volume 3, 913.
39. Letter to Pownall, October 3, 1775.

very infirm father-in-law—evidently no very welcome guest.[40] He was never to see Elizabeth Rogers again. Proceeding toward his farm at Rumford, he passed by way of Hanover, where he stopped for dinner at the cultured home of the Rev. Eleazar Wheelock, head of the struggling young college there—one of the most interesting interviews of his whole career. He did not impress the venerable minister and educator favourably. In faded undress uniform, he was uncouth and ill-restrained in manner, while his splendid physique already showed evidence of wreck and dissipation. He talked boastfully of his services in Africa, of his large grants of land, and of flattering offers which he had rejected from the provincial army, and officiously volunteered to assist Dr. Wheelock in obtaining English aid for his institution—a proposal which was coldly declined. All Rogers' movements were by this time regarded with suspicion by colonial patriots, and next day the minister addressed to Washington at Cambridge a full account of their meeting.[41]

Meanwhile, having economically avoided payment of his night's lodging at a neighbouring inn, the shabby major had fared on to his farm; and from thence he set out again, in the course of a week, to return to the British headquarters at New York. Two interesting occurrences marked his homeward journey. On his way to Medford he fell in with a tall, alert lad of fifteen, and, struck by his appearance, engaged him in conversation. Finding that the boy was the son of his old fellow in the ranging service, Captain John Stark, on his way to join his father in camp, he paid his reckoning at the hostelry at which they stopped at noon. That night at Medford he held a long conversation with the elder Stark, and drew from him a declaration of his unfaltering allegiance to the American cause.[42] The second incident was concerned with a more eminent continental officer. The next day, December 14th, he sent a letter by Stark to

40. Some doubt may be thrown upon his story of the fever and ague by his wife's testimony that "he was in a situation which, as her peace and safety forced her to shun and fly from him, so decency forbids her to say more upon so indelicate a subject." Petition to the New Hampshire General Assembly, 1778.
41. *American Archives,* Series 4, Volume 4, 158.
42. Hurd, *History of Merrimac County,* p. 302.

Washington in the latter's entrenchments before Boston, asking for a continuance of his permit to pursue his private affairs, as he believed it would require some months yet for him to settle with his creditors. "I have leave to retire on my half-pay, and never expect to be called in service again." he added. "I love North America; it is my native country; and I expect to spend the evening of my days in it."[43]

This at last was conscious duplicity, for he was even then in hopes of a fresh commission. Washington's single decisive answer was to order General Schuyler to keep a close watch over the ranger, and to make arrangements for a constant return of information concerning his motions. On January 5, 1776, by the first of these reports, the commander-in-chief learned that the major had set out from Albany to New York.[44] On the very same day Lord Germain, three thousand miles away, wrote to General George Howe, cousin of the young subaltern who had known Rogers in the Seven Years War, and now Gage's successor as head of the British army: "The king approves of the arrangement you propose in respect to an adjutant-general and a quartermaster-general, and your attention to Major Rogers, of whose firmness and fidelity we have received further testimony from Governor Tryon."[45] As the one cause treated him with suspicion and disdain, the other courted his assistance.

Rogers, however, was still to wait some trying months for his appointment; for his business in the middle colonies remained unfinished, and it was impossible for him in any event to join Howe, closely pent with an unaggressive army within Boston. He busied himself chiefly about New York, free to come and go in its streets as he pleased, but under a supervision that grew daily harsher and more minute. The city was become so patriot that Governor Tryon and his council had been forced to flee aboard the British ship *Asia* in the harbour, and the Tory ele-

---

43. *American Archives,* Series 4, Volume 4, 265.
44. *American Archives,* Series 4, Volume 4, 581.
45. *Idem,* p. 575. Gage had sailed for England October 10th, 1775. It was advised by the ministry that Howe continue the war from New York, but he remained at Boston.

ments in the population concealed their sentiments and their hopes in meekness and fear.[46] The half-pay major, still lodging on Broadway, felt with many others the severity of the party feeling manifested by the Whigs, and of the radical restriction imposed by the great numbers who were now beginning openly to express their hopes of an immediate declaration of independence. In the preceding August, the Provincial Congress of New York had resolved to punish by imprisonment and forfeiture of property those who gave information or supplies to the enemy; in September it had authorized the seizure of the arms of all those who had not sworn allegiance to the American cause; and throughout the winter it saw that the local committees of safety kept a minute watch over such suspects as Rogers. In his business operations the major felt especially hampered. During February, 1776, while he was still soliciting grants of several tracts of land within the province, he was forced to petition the Provincial Congress for permission to attend "his excellency the governor" on board the *Duchess of Gordon,* then lying with four other warships between Nutter's and Bedloe's Islands, and not until he had carefully specified that it was "business of a private nature, and such only as respects myself and creditors," that rendered his attendance aboard ship necessary, was he given the requested permit.[47]

With the coming of the colonial army a few weeks later his situation grew doubly irksome and dangerous. On March 4th, 1776, the American commander-in-chief had fortified Dorchester Heights, with the result that within ten days Howe evacuated Boston, and, abandoning all his stores, set sail with his troops and more than a thousand Massachusetts loyalists for Nova Scotia. The continental headquarters were at once removed southward. On April 13th, Washington arrived at New York, and for many days thereafter his ragged, ill-fed, but faithful troops came straggling in over the rough, muddy spring roads to the port. Neither he nor his men had any sympathy for American-born citizens

---

46. For this and other general matter see C. H. Van Tyne, *The American Revolution* (Volume 9 of *The American Nation: A History*), New York, 1905.

47. *American Archives,* Series 4, Volume 4, 1201.

who still adhered to the British cause, and living as they were in daily fear of an English naval attack, they took prompt measures to drive out or chain up intestine enemies. "Why," asked Washington, "should persons who are preying upon the vitals of the country be suffered to stalk at large, whilst we know that they will do every mischief in their power?"[48]

The next few weeks were weeks of terror to all loyalists, for they were harried by the militia, seized and imprisoned without mercy, or sent in exile to neighbouring colonies upon parole.[49] None of them was an object of greater suspicion than Rogers, and none was made more clearly to feel the uneasy sufferance with which his presence was regarded. Immediately before leaving Cambridge, Washington wrote Schuyler at Albany that: "Rogers being much suspected of unfriendly views toward this country, his conduct should be attended to with some degree of vigilance and circumspection,"[50] and at his arrival he detailed Captain Peters of the New York colonials to preserve a close watch over all his goings and comings, and saw to it that sources of information concerning his actions in New Hampshire and New York were probed.

His vigilance was not without fruit, for Rogers was utterly unable to maintain a plausible and innocent appearance. He went north on business again in the late spring; and in returning in June from the oversight of his property at Rumford, he followed so vagrant a course that he was taken up at South Amboy, New Jersey, and examined in council by Washington, Greene, Stirling, Mifflin, and other colonial generals. He was strongly suspected of activity as a spy, and implausibly pleaded to the commanders that he had gone out of his way only to make a secret offer of his services to Continental Congress, showing as proof various commendatory letters which he had secured from American friends. The council, however, resolved that he was too dangerous a character to be permitted to enter the revolutionary ranks, and Washington sent him on to

---

48. *Washington's Writings,* Sparks' edition, III, 357.
49. *Calendar of New York Historical Mss.,* I, 338.
50. American Archives, Series 4, Volume 4, 696.

his destination with a letter recommending that a deaf ear be turned to his proffer. The step was a wise one, for at the same moment (June 25th) the New Hampshire House of Representatives was appointing a committee to "consider the expediency of securing Major Rogers in consequence of sundry informations against him." Under conduct of a guard detailed from Washington's camp, the major was transmitted to Philadelphia in the closing days of June; and thus he was present a prisoner, lying in the very shadow of Independence Hill, at the birth of the United States.[51]

When he arrived on July 1st, Philadelphia already felt a premonition of the great event. Hancock announced the inception of the measure and Rogers' coming in the same letter to Washington. "Major Rogers is under guard the barracks," he wrote, "congress having, by a particular appointment, had under consideration a momentous matter this day, which prevented their attention to him. My next will inform you, I hope, of some very decisive measures."[52]

The momentous matter of which he spoke was Richard Henry Lee's motion that "These united colonies are, and of right ought to be, free and independent states." Discussion upon it and upon Jefferson's draft of the declaration wholly engrossed the next three days. It was not until July 5th, when the important step had been debated and determined upon, adopted by twelve colonies, and signed by the president and secretary, that the major, waiting to know his fate, was given a moment's consideration. It was summarily ordered by Congress that he be sent to the New Hampshire Assembly for final disposal. This reference of the case was notified to the provincial body in the same letter of Hancock's, dated July 6th, which, after prefacing that "although it is not possible to foresee the consequences of human actions, yet it is nevertheless a duty which we owe to ourselves and posterity, in all our public councils, to decide the best we are able, and trust the event of God," heralded the dissolution of the connection between the colonies and Great

51. *American Archives,* Series 4, Volume 6, 1108, 1109.
52. *Idem,* Volume 6, 1108. *Idem,* series 5, Volume I, 33.

Britain.[53] But Rogers had no intention of answering for his alleged informations and treacheries, and in the early morning of July 8th, while still held under a loose guard at Philadelphia, found means to make his escape. The Pennsylvania Committee of Safety offered a reward of £50 for his head, but he safely made his way across country to Staten Island, where Howe, with thirty thousand men, had just landed.[54]

Here Rogers was received with open arms. Not merely had Howe been assured of his ability and held previous communication with him, but to an army composed largely of men untrained in New World methods of fighting, unfamiliar with the enemy, and entirely uncertain of the ground over which it must pass, he seemed, a valuable accession. He knew intimately the whole central region along the Hudson and toward Philadelphia in which Howe was to operate, and the temper and immediate resources of the Americans; and he had many Tory friends in the neighbouring boroughs whom he could induce to enter the British army. In the first days of August, he was given the title of lieutenant-colonel, and empowered to muster a battalion of loyalists, to be called the Queen's American Rangers.[55]

It was only in the first campaign after he joined the British army, however—the campaign of the autumn and winter of 1776-7, along the lower course of the Hudson, and through New Jersey—that Rogers' connection with the American Revolution was one of any importance. The earliest movements about New York demonstrated that, however successful he had been in partisan fighting, he had little place in an army which marched, deployed, and fought in European style, over ground for the most part well-cleared and cultivated, and under generals who realized all the advantages of a complicated system of military tactics. During Howe's preliminary manoeuvres to drive Washington out of the city, he was fortunately occupied in collecting his men, whom he drew from all the towns in lower

---

53. *American Archives*, Series 5, Volume I, 33.
54. *Idem*, p. 136.
55. For a first hand history of this battalion see *The Queen's Rangers* by John Simcoe, published by Leonaur.

Connecticut, Long Island, and along the New York shore of the Sound. His method of enlistment was that time-honoured and serviceable one by which he offered a commission to a chosen few who engaged to bring in a certain quota of soldiers; a method which, while it rapidly filled his ranks, at the same time gave him a corps of officers notable chiefly for their inefficiency. His allotment of four hundred men made up, he was sent to occupy that position along the front where it was expected his force of pickets and scouts would prove of especial service. While he was enlisting his troops, Howe had won the battle of Long Island, and forced Washington successively from Brooklyn Heights to New York, and from New York to White Plains, half-way to the Connecticut line. It was in the attempt to defeat him here during October that the commander of the Queen's Rangers saw his first active fighting of the war.

On the twelfth of October, Howe landed a large force of men ten miles up the East River, and urged them forward as rapidly as possible past Forts Lee and Washington, while he simultaneously disembarked Rogers and others on the shore of the Sound, hoping to cut off the communication of the continental army with Connecticut.

Rogers, stationed with his battalion during the past fortnight at Huntington on Long Island, had for some time been meditating a descent[56] upon the colonial stores collected at Greenwich, Stamford, and Norwalk, with the inlets and avenues to which his men were perfectly familiar. Now, shielding his eastern wing with the Queen's Rangers, the commander-in-chief at once began to explore along the whole front the possibility for a general advance. As Rogers' outpost party was moved forward toward White Plains, the force which he commanded finally took a bold station at Mamaroneck, only ten miles distant from the American lines.

Here, on the night of October 21st, he was attacked by a regiment of nearly double his own numbers, under Colonel Haslett, who inflicted upon his men a defeat so crushing that only

---

56. *American Archives*, series 5, Volume 2, 1208.

the darkness, and the defection of some of the American guards, prevented their annihilation. As it was, they took thirty-six prisoners, a pair of colours, and many arms and provisions, and drove back the boasted new corps in humiliating disorder.[57]

Stirling was so pleased with Haslett's success that he thanked him and his men publicly on parade. The new hatred and contempt of the patriots for Rogers is felt in every letter reporting the affair. "The late worthless major skulked off in the dark," says one; another speaks of him as characteristically "very careful to get himself off, though he often leaves his men in the lurch."[58] The whole action was but a skirmish, however, and with Washington's defeat at White Plains a week later, the war was carried southwest toward Philadelphia.

Thus briefly and ingloriously was Rogers' revolutionary career, to all practical purposes, ended. A few weeks later the leadership of his corps was given to Colonel French, and then to Major Wemyss; until finally, on October 15, 1777, it passed to Major J. G. Simcoe, who dismissed the more incompetent officers, substituted southerners for them, and brought the command to a high state of efficiency.[59] Henceforth the now more and more discredited major, apparently kept in service chiefly by the memory of his past achievements, was employed only as a recruiting officer.

In October, 1778, he still preserved some connection with his corps, for at Quebec he petitioned Haldimand, Governor of Canada, to be permitted to rejoin it at New York by way of England, the only route then open, and actually signed himself as its ranking officer. At the same time he was seeking employment at the north, for Haldimand refused as impracticable his petition to be allowed to raise two battalions from the neighbouring colonies. He was permitted, however, to return for a brief space to the mother country, where he still had. matters of business.

His stay in England was brief, although we learn from a letter he later sent to the governor, thanking him for his leave of

---

57. *American Archives,* Series 5, Volume 2, 1270.
58. *Idem,* pp. 1187 and 1270.
59. See the introduction to Simcoe's *The Queen's Rangers,* published by Leonaur.

absence, that through it he "found means to get provided for." On May 1st, 1779, he was back to New York. Here he secured authority from Clinton to attempt the recruiting for which Haldimand had withheld permission, men being sadly needed by the British army, and immediately sent out officers to begin enlistments in the northern communities contiguous with the Canadian border.[60] Each battalion was to be commanded by a major, who would issue his orders, when the ranks were full, through nine captains to six hundred men.

One of the recruiting agents for whom-the major happily secured employment was his brother, Major James Rogers, who had been totally ruined by the confiscation of his wealthy estate in Vermont, and driven by the rapacious and vindictive Whigs from his wife and six children into Canada.[61] Rogers appointed him major of one of the two battalions, and in May, 1780, petitioned Haldimand to create him also lieutenant-colonel. He, and one or two of Rogers other subordinates, proved effective servants, and the corps was shortly put upon a foundation which augured a speedy organization.

By this period of the war, indeed, the ranger had become known as one of the most prominent and active of the various leaders who drew loyalist volunteers into George Ill's army, and for his pertinacity in northern New Hampshire had been proscribed in November, 1778, by the representatives of his old colony.[62] His headquarters he established first at St. John s, New Brunswick, and later at Kamouraska, Quebec, and successfully began to prosecute his enlistments for the King's Rangers, as the new troop was to be called, along the "eastern frontiers of New England and Penobscot." In the autumn of 1779, having halted for a few days at Penobscot harbour, he witnessed there a small naval battle.[63]

---

60. For the remainder of the references to Rogers services as a recruiting officer see the *Canadian Archives*, 1888, Haldimand Collection, pp. 673-6837.

61. In the *Proceedings of the Royal Society of Canada*, Series II, Volume 6, is an account of James Rogers by one of his descendants. His estate in what is now Windham County, Vermont, was valued at £30,000, and comprised 22,000 acres. After the war he received a township in the Frontenac district of Ontario. There is no doubt that he was a man of both integrity and ability. He died in 1792.

62. New Hampshire State Papers, VIII, 810. (continued on next page)

Had he held to his new task with the energy with which he entered upon it—had he even permitted his brother James to prosecute it without hindrance or help from himself, Rogers might successfully have weathered the few remaining storms that could have lowered about him before the conclusion of the war, and retired from it with scarcely less honour than the generality of English officers. He was now fifty years old, a veteran in the service. The two enemies that were to interpose themselves, however, were those which he had no genius to conquer—dishonesty, and his old, drunken, threadbare vices of everyday life. His semi-authoritative and detached position, allowing him to spend much time in Quebec, Montreal, and New York; his want of direct responsibility to any superior officer; his cutting-off from the vigorously hurried life of the army in the held, which alone was sufficient to keep him from liquor and gambling, all conspired to one end. His time was wasted, his duties neglected, his ready money laid waste and that of his brother and his department peculated, even while the dragging war revealed new resources and determination on the part of the Americans, and called with more urgency for the men he might have sent.

In September, 1779, Rogers reported to Haldimand at Quebec that he had raised seven hundred men, for whose expenses, with his own, he sent in a requisition for £500. His success elicited general congratulation; which abruptly ceased when in the early spring, it having become necessary to move these troops forward, it appeared that their number had unaccountably dropped to forty.

Meanwhile, the major had spent the winter months in Que-

63. One battalion of the King's Rangers was destined for service in Quebec Province, the other at Halifax. Rogers' commission to the command of the corps was dated May 1st, 1779, his brother James was gazetted Major June 2nd, 1779. Eleven other newly-appointed officers were sent northward on the brigantine *Hawk* arriving at Montreal in September, 1779; Rogers, following with his own staff on the sloop *Bloud*, happened to be at Penobscot on August 13th, the day the British won a small naval victory there. The total strength of the Canadian army was then six thousand men. For a time much confusion was caused by the fact that Haldimand was given no definite instructions as to the embodiment of the new corps. Finally, on his own authority, he placed it upon a half-pay establishment of his own. *Proceedings of the Royal Society of Canada*, Series II, Volume 6, Section 2, p. 49

bec, where he drew money on the accounts of his subordinate officers, and spent it in drunken and riotous revellings. One lieutenant, named Longstreet, whom he thus cheated of £25, was especially bitter against him, and complained loudly to Haldimand. In March he was deeper than ever in his evil courses, and the governor found difficulty in getting him to return to the front; he reprimanded Rogers severely when, ten days after the major had announced his departure, and drawn money and other necessities for his journey, an aide found him still skulking about the streets of the town.

When finally he set out for Kamouraska, he "contracted debts and drew bills the whole way," as Haldimand's secretary tells us, and "thoroughly disgraced and injured the whole cause." It had become evident by this time that it would be suicidal to the British hopes of drawing many volunteers from the loyalists along the northern frontier to permit so disreputable an officer to remain in charge of the enlistment.

On March 20th, Rogers wrote from the Lac du Grand-Portage, on his way south, that he hoped "his excellency will overlook anything wherein I have given offense, as I have nothing more at heart than his majesty's service." He was immediately made to realize, however, that his best safety lay in a complete evasion of Haldimand's condemnation. On April 26th, 1780, he fled to Halifax to board a ship, on which he sailed for England a few days later; writing his brother James on the eve of his departure that he was sorry his affairs were in such confusion, and that he would send an agent back to America to arrange for meeting his financial obligations.

In July, there came as a last echo of his service a number of bills which he had contracted at Kamouraska; they were drawn on his brother James, whom they left financially prostrate, while as a humiliation of the Canadian organization for recruiting they thoroughly angered Haldimand. Rogers, however, still retained his command, for his commission had been issued by Clinton, and it was not in Haldimand's power to revoke it; and even James, sensitive under the stigma of his brother's disgrace, unable to meet any fresh debts drawn upon the Kings Rangers, and moreover embroiled in disagreeable quarrels with officers enlisting for rival branches, was unable to resign his post and take a fresh commission under Haldimand himself. After several futile attempts at escape, he devoted himself manfully to his task of completing the Rangers, beset by manifold jealousies and difficulties, and when the war was over had rostered and equipped four companies. The promised agent from his brother never came to assist him, and of course Robert Rogers himself never touched American soil again. The last full reference to him written on this continent is in a letter of his brother's, bearing a date virtually coincident with his departure:

> The conduct of my brother of late had almost unmanned me. When I was last in Quebec I often wrote to and told him my mind in regard to it, and as often he promised to reform. I am sorry his good talents should so unguarded fall a prey to intemperance.

On May 18, 1795, Rogers died in poor lodgings in a populous and busy part of south London.[64] Of the conduct of his life after leaving Halifax fifteen years before we know nothing. There is a tradition in his family, recorded in every account of the ranger's career, but unsupported by any contemporary evidence, that his last years were improvident and vicious—a tradition in full harmony with our knowledge of his character and tendencies at the time of his return to England. That they were also accompanied by the disease and infirmity that his evil habits and once great hardships had ensured there can be little doubt. Our only means of tracing his continued existence, however, lies in the fact that after the conclusion of peace with the United States in 1783 his name occurs regularly on the half-pay registers, where he is credited with a daily stipend of eight shillings five pence, a sum ample for the maintenance of life in comfort.

He never left the city, and, dying where he had lived, in the parish of Newington Butts, was buried five days later in the grounds of the old church of St. Mary Newington. His grave

---

64. *Paymaster-General's Books*, 1795.

is now unknown; for the church has been torn down and the churchyard paved over. He left no will, and his estate, valued at but £100, was assigned to John Walker, a creditor.[65] No one, so far as we know, mourned his going. His wife had been divorced[66] from him by a decree of the New Hampshire legislature, seventeen years before, and—she having remarried—his only son had grown up under an alien roof, among patriot Americans who regarded all loyalists with opprobrium

Rogers died in total obscurity, and no newspaper or newsletter, in either America, or England, chronicled his going in its curtest list of obituaries.

---

65. *Administration Act Book*, 1796.

66. This divorce was granted by legislative action on March 4, 1778. *New Hampshire State Papers,* VIII, 776. After her divorce Elizabeth Rogers married Captain John Roach, a retired British sea-captain, living with him upon the Rogers estate just outside Concord until her death in 1812. The land and the old house descended to her son Arthur Rogers, who after living many years in Portsmouth, and practising law there, 1793-4, died there in 1841, leaving three children in respectable standing in San Domingo.

LEONAUR
ALSO FROM LEONAUR
AVAILABLE IN SOFTCOVER OR HARDCOVER WITH DUST JACKET

THE 2ND MAORI WAR: 1860-1861 *by Robert Carey*—The Second Maori War, or First Taranaki War, one more bloody instalment of the conflicts between European settlers and the indigenous Maori people.

A JOURNAL OF THE SECOND SIKH WAR *by Daniel A. Sandford*—The Experiences of an Ensign of the 2nd Bengal European Regiment During the Campaign in the Punjab, India, 1848-49.

THE LIGHT INFANTRY OFFICER *by John H. Cooke*—The Experiences of an Officer of the 43rd Light Infantry in America During the War of 1812.

BUSHVELDT CARBINEERS *by George Witton*—The War Against the Boers in South Africa and the 'Breaker' Morant Incident.

LAKE'S CAMPAIGNS IN INDIA *by Hugh Pearse*—The Second Anglo Maratha War, 1803-1807.

BRITAIN IN AFGHANISTAN 1: THE FIRST AFGHAN WAR 1839-42 *by Archibald Forbes*—From invasion to destruction-a British military disaster.

BRITAIN IN AFGHANISTAN 2: THE SECOND AFGHAN WAR 1878-80 *by Archibald Forbes*—This is the history of the Second Afghan War-another episode of British military history typified by savagery, massacre, siege and battles.

UP AMONG THE PANDIES *by Vivian Dering Majendie*—Experiences of a British Officer on Campaign During the Indian Mutiny, 1857-1858.

MUTINY: 1857 *by James Humphries*—Authentic Voices from the Indian Mutiny-First Hand Accounts of Battles, Sieges and Personal Hardships.

BLOW THE BUGLE, DRAW THE SWORD *by W. H. G. Kingston*—The Wars, Campaigns, Regiments and Soldiers of the British & Indian Armies During the Victorian Era, 1839-1898.

WAR BEYOND THE DRAGON PAGODA *by Major J. J. Snodgrass*—A Personal Narrative of the First Anglo-Burmese War 1824 - 1826.

THE HERO OF ALIWAL *by James Humphries*—The Campaigns of Sir Harry Smith in India, 1843-1846, During the Gwalior War & the First Sikh War.

ALL FOR A SHILLING A DAY *by Donald F. Featherstone*—The story of H.M. 16th, the Queen's Lancers During the first Sikh War 1845-1846.

LEONAUR

ALSO FROM LEONAUR
AVAILABLE IN SOFTCOVER OR HARDCOVER WITH DUST JACKET

THE FALL OF THE MOGHUL EMPIRE OF HINDUSTAN by H. G. Keene—
By the beginning of the nineteenth century, as British and Indian armies under Lake
and Wellesley dominated the scene, a little over half a century of conflict brought the
Moghul Empire to its knees.

LADY SALE'S AFGHANISTAN by Florentia Sale—An Indomitable Victorian
Lady's Account of the Retreat from Kabul During the First Afghan War.

THE CAMPAIGN OF MAGENTA AND SOLFERINO 1859 by Harold Car-
michael Wylly—The Decisive Conflict for the Unification of Italy.

FRENCH'S CAVALRY CAMPAIGN by J. G. Maydon—A Special Correspo-
nent's View of British Army Mounted Troops During the Boer War.

CAVALRY AT WATERLOO by Sir Evelyn Wood—British Mounted Troops
During the Campaign of 1815.

THE SUBALTERN by George Robert Gleig—The Experiences of an Officer of
the 85th Light Infantry During the Peninsular War.

NAPOLEON AT BAY, 1814 by F. Loraine Petre—The Campaigns to the Fall of
the First Empire.

NAPOLEON AND THE CAMPAIGN OF 1806 by Colonel Vachée—The Napoleonic Method of Organisation and Command to the Battles of Jena & Auerstädt.

THE COMPLETE ADVENTURES IN THE CONNAUGHT RANGERS by
William Grattan—The 88th Regiment during the Napoleonic Wars by a Serving
Officer.

BUGLER AND OFFICER OF THE RIFLES by William Green & Harry
Smith—With the 95th (Rifles) during the Peninsular & Waterloo Campaigns of the
Napoleonic Wars.

NAPOLEONIC WAR STORIES by Sir Arthur Quiller-Couch—Tales of soldiers,
spies, battles & sieges from the Peninsular & Waterloo campaingns.

CAPTAIN OF THE 95TH (RIFLES) by Jonathan Leach—An officer of Wellington's sharpshooters during the Peninsular, South of France and Waterloo campaigns of the Napoleonic wars.

RIFLEMAN COSTELLO by Edward Costello—The adventures of a soldier of
the 95th (Rifles) in the Peninsular & Waterloo Campaigns of the Napoleonic wars.

LEONAUR

ALSO FROM LEONAUR
AVAILABLE IN SOFTCOVER OR HARDCOVER WITH DUST JACKET

ADVENTURES OF A YOUNG RIFLEMAN *by Johann Christian Maempel*—The Experiences of a Saxon in the French & British Armies During the Napoleonic Wars.

THE HUSSAR *by Norbert Landsheit & G. R. Gleig*—A German Cavalryman in British Service Throughout the Napoleonic Wars.

RECOLLECTIONS OF THE PENINSULA *by Moyle Sherer*—An Officer of the 34th Regiment of Foot—'The Cumberland Gentlemen'—on Campaign Against Napoleon's French Army in Spain.

MARINE OF REVOLUTION & CONSULATE *by Moreau de Jonnès*—The Recollections of a French Soldier of the Revolutionary Wars 1791-1804.

GENTLEMEN IN RED *by John Dobbs & Robert Knowles*—Two Accounts of British Infantry Officers During the Peninsular War Recollections of an Old 52nd Man by John Dobbs An Officer of Fusiliers by Robert Knowles.

CORPORAL BROWN'S CAMPAIGNS IN THE LOW COUNTRIES *by Robert Brown*—Recollections of a Coldstream Guard in the Early Campaigns Against Revolutionary France 1793-1795.

THE 7TH (QUEENS OWN) HUSSARS: Volume 2—1793-1815 *by C. R. B. Barrett*—During the Campaigns in the Low Countries & the Peninsula and Waterloo Campaigns of the Napoleonic Wars. Volume 2: 1793-1815.

THE MARENGO CAMPAIGN 1800 *by Herbert H. Sargent*—The Victory that Completed the Austrian Defeat in Italy.

DONALDSON OF THE 94TH—SCOTS BRIGADE *by Joseph Donaldson*—The Recollections of a Soldier During the Peninsula & South of France Campaigns of the Napoleonic Wars.

A CONSCRIPT FOR EMPIRE *by Philippe as told to Johann Christian Maempel*—The Experiences of a Young German Conscript During the Napoleonic Wars.

JOURNAL OF THE CAMPAIGN OF 1815 *by Alexander Cavalié Mercer*—The Experiences of an Officer of the Royal Horse Artillery During the Waterloo Campaign.

NAPOLEON'S CAMPAIGNS IN POLAND 1806-7 *by Robert Wilson*—The campaign in Poland from the Russian side of the conflict.

LEONAUR

ALSO FROM LEONAUR

AVAILABLE IN SOFTCOVER OR HARDCOVER WITH DUST JACKET

CAPTAIN COIGNET *by Jean-Roch Coignet*—A Soldier of Napoleon's Imperial Guard from the Italian Campaign to Russia and Waterloo.

HUSSAR ROCCA *by Albert Jean Michel de Rocca*—A French cavalry officer's experiences of the Napoleonic Wars and his views on the Peninsular Campaigns against the Spanish, British And Guerilla Armies.

MARINES TO 95TH (RIFLES) *by Thomas Fernyhough*—The military experiences of Robert Fernyhough during the Napoleonic Wars.

LIGHT BOB *by Robert Blakeney*—The experiences of a young officer in H.M 28th & 36th regiments of the British Infantry during the Peninsular Campaign of the Napoleonic Wars 1804 - 1814.

WITH WELLINGTON'S LIGHT CAVALRY *by William Tomkinson*—The Experiences of an officer of the 16th Light Dragoons in the Peninsular and Waterloo campaigns of the Napoleonic Wars.

SERGEANT BOURGOGNE *by Adrien Bourgogne*—With Napoleon's Imperial Guard in the Russian Campaign and on the Retreat from Moscow 1812 - 13.

SURTEES OF THE 95TH (RIFLES) *by William Surtees*—A Soldier of the 95th (Rifles) in the Peninsular campaign of the Napoleonic Wars.

SWORDS OF HONOUR *by Henry Newbolt & Stanley L. Wood*—The Careers of Six Outstanding Officers from the Napoleonic Wars, the Wars for India and the American Civil War.

ENSIGN BELL IN THE PENINSULAR WAR *by George Bell*—The Experiences of a young British Soldier of the 34th Regiment 'The Cumberland Gentlemen' in the Napoleonic wars.

HUSSAR IN WINTER *by Alexander Gordon*—A British Cavalry Officer during the retreat to Corunna in the Peninsular campaign of the Napoleonic Wars.

THE COMPLEAT RIFLEMAN HARRIS *by Benjamin Harris as told to and transcribed by Captain Henry Curling, 52nd Regt. of Foot*—The adventures of a soldier of the 95th (Rifles) during the Peninsular Campaign of the Napoleonic Wars.

THE ADVENTURES OF A LIGHT DRAGOON *by George Farmer & G.R. Gleig*—A cavalryman during the Peninsular & Waterloo Campaigns, in captivity & at the siege of Bhurtpore, India.

ALSO FROM LEONAUR
AVAILABLE IN SOFTCOVER OR HARDCOVER WITH DUST JACKET

THE RELUCTANT REBEL *by William G. Stevenson*—A young Kentuckian's experiences in the Confederate Infantry & Cavalry during the American Civil War..

BOOTS AND SADDLES *by Elizabeth B. Custer*—The experiences of General Custer's Wife on the Western Plains.

FANNIE BEERS' CIVIL WAR *by Fannie A. Beers*—A Confederate Lady's Experiences of Nursing During the Campaigns & Battles of the American Civil War.

LADY SALE'S AFGHANISTAN *by Florentia Sale*—An Indomitable Victorian Lady's Account of the Retreat from Kabul During the First Afghan War.

THE TWO WARS OF MRS DUBERLY *by Frances Isabella Duberly*—An Intrepid Victorian Lady's Experience of the Crimea and Indian Mutiny.

THE REBELLIOUS DUCHESS *by Paul F. S. Dermoncourt*—The Adventures of the Duchess of Berri and Her Attempt to Overthrow French Monarchy.

LADIES OF WATERLOO *by Charlotte A. Eaton, Magdalene de Lancey & Juana Smith*—The Experiences of Three Women During the Campaign of 1815: Waterloo Days by Charlotte A. Eaton, A Week at Waterloo by Magdalene de Lancey & Juana's Story by Juana Smith.

TWO YEARS BEFORE THE MAST *by Richard Henry Dana. Jr.*—The account of one young man's experiences serving on board a sailing brig—the Penelope—bound for California, between the years1834-36.

A SAILOR OF KING GEORGE *by Frederick Hoffman*—From Midshipman to Captain—Recollections of War at Sea in the Napoleonic Age 1793-1815.

LORDS OF THE SEA *by A. T. Mahan*—Great Captains of the Royal Navy During the Age of Sail.

COGGESHALL'S VOYAGES: VOLUME 1 *by George Coggeshall*—The Recollections of an American Schooner Captain.

COGGESHALL'S VOYAGES: VOLUME 2 *by George Coggeshall*—The Recollections of an American Schooner Captain.

TWILIGHT OF EMPIRE *by Sir Thomas Ussher & Sir George Cockburn*—Two accounts of Napoleon's Journeys in Exile to Elba and St. Helena: Narrative of Events by Sir Thomas Ussher & Napoleon's Last Voyage: Extract of a diary by Sir George Cockburn.

LEONAUR

ALSO FROM LEONAUR
AVAILABLE IN SOFTCOVER OR HARDCOVER WITH DUST JACKET

ESCAPE FROM THE FRENCH by Edward Boys—A Young Royal Navy Midshipman's Adventures During the Napoleonic War.

THE VOYAGE OF H.M.S. PANDORA by Edward Edwards R. N. & George Hamilton, edited by Basil Thomson—In Pursuit of the Mutineers of the Bounty in the South Seas—1790-1791.

MEDUSA by J. B. Henry Savigny and Alexander Correard and Charlotte-Adélaïde Dard —Narrative of a Voyage to Senegal in 1816 & The Sufferings of the Picard Family After the Shipwreck of the Medusa.

THE SEA WAR OF 1812 VOLUME 1 by A. T. Mahan—A History of the Maritime Conflict.

THE SEA WAR OF 1812 VOLUME 2 by A. T. Mahan—A History of the Maritime Conflict.

WETHERELL OF H. M. S. HUSSAR by John Wetherell—The Recollections of an Ordinary Seaman of the Royal Navy During the Napoleonic Wars.

THE NAVAL BRIGADE IN NATAL by C. R. N. Burne—With the Guns of H. M. S. Terrible & H. M. S. Tartar during the Boer War 1899-1900.

THE VOYAGE OF H. M. S. BOUNTY by William Bligh—The True Story of an 18th Century Voyage of Exploration and Mutiny.

SHIPWRECK! by William Gilly—The Royal Navy's Disasters at Sea 1793-1849.

KING'S CUTTERS AND SMUGGLERS: 1700-1855 by E. Keble Chatterton—A unique period of maritime history-from the beginning of the eighteenth to the middle of the nineteenth century when British seamen risked all to smuggle valuable goods from wool to tea and spirits from and to the Continent.

CONFEDERATE BLOCKADE RUNNER by John Wilkinson—The Personal Recollections of an Officer of the Confederate Navy.

NAVAL BATTLES OF THE NAPOLEONIC WARS by W. H. Fitchett—Cape St. Vincent, the Nile, Cadiz, Copenhagen, Trafalgar & Others.

PRISONERS OF THE RED DESERT by R. S. Gwatkin-Williams—The Adventures of the Crew of the Tara During the First World War.

U-BOAT WAR 1914-1918 by James B. Connolly/Karl von Schenk—Two Contrasting Accounts from Both Sides of the Conflict at Sea D uring the Great War.

LEONAUR

ALSO FROM LEONAUR
AVAILABLE IN SOFTCOVER OR HARDCOVER WITH DUST JACKET

IRON TIMES WITH THE GUARDS *by An O. E. (G. P. A. Fildes)*—The Experiences of an Officer of the Coldstream Guards on the Western Front During the First World War.

THE GREAT WAR IN THE MIDDLE EAST: 1 *by W. T. Massey*—The Desert Campaigns & How Jerusalem Was Won---two classic accounts in one volume.

THE GREAT WAR IN THE MIDDLE EAST: 2 *by W. T. Massey*—Allenby's Final Triumph.

SMITH-DORRIEN *by Horace Smith-Dorrien*—Isandlwhana to the Great War.

1914 *by Sir John French*—The Early Campaigns of the Great War by the British Commander.

GRENADIER *by E. R. M. Fryer*—The Recollections of an Officer of the Grenadier Guards throughout the Great War on the Western Front.

BATTLE, CAPTURE & ESCAPE *by George Pearson*—The Experiences of a Canadian Light Infantryman During the Great War.

DIGGERS AT WAR *by R. Hugh Knyvett & G. P. Cuttriss*—"Over There" With the Australians by R. Hugh Knyvett and Over the Top With the Third Australian Division by G. P. Cuttriss. Accounts of Australians During the Great War in the Middle East, at Gallipoli and on the Western Front.

HEAVY FIGHTING BEFORE US *by George Brenton Laurie*—The Letters of an Officer of the Royal Irish Rifles on the Western Front During the Great War.

THE CAMELIERS *by Oliver Hogue*—A Classic Account of the Australians of the Imperial Camel Corps During the First World War in the Middle East.

RED DUST *by Donald Black*—A Classic Account of Australian Light Horsemen in Palestine During the First World War.

THE LEAN, BROWN MEN *by Angus Buchanan*—Experiences in East Africa During the Great War with the 25th Royal Fusiliers—the Legion of Frontiersmen.

THE NIGERIAN REGIMENT IN EAST AFRICA *by W. D. Downes*—On Campaign During the Great War 1916-1918.

THE 'DIE-HARDS' IN SIBERIA *by John Ward*—With the Middlesex Regiment Against the Bolsheviks 1918-19.

LEONAUR

ALSO FROM LEONAUR
AVAILABLE IN SOFTCOVER OR HARDCOVER WITH DUST JACKET

THE 9TH—THE KING'S (LIVERPOOL REGIMENT) IN THE GREAT WAR 1914 - 1918 *by Enos H. G. Roberts*—Mersey to mud—war and Liverpool men.

THE GAMBARDIER *by Mark Severn*—The experiences of a battery of Heavy artillery on the Western Front during the First World War.

FROM MESSINES TO THIRD YPRES *by Thomas Floyd*—A personal account of the First World War on the Western front by a 2/5th Lancashire Fusilier.

THE IRISH GUARDS IN THE GREAT WAR - VOLUME 1 *by Rudyard Kipling*—Edited and Compiled from Their Diaries and Papers—The First Battalion.

THE IRISH GUARDS IN THE GREAT WAR - VOLUME 1 *by Rudyard Kipling*—Edited and Compiled from Their Diaries and Papers—The Second Battalion.

ARMOURED CARS IN EDEN *by K. Roosevelt*—An American President's son serving in Rolls Royce armoured cars with the British in Mesopatamia & with the American Artillery in France during the First World War.

CHASSEUR OF 1914 *by Marcel Dupont*—Experiences of the twilight of the French Light Cavalry by a young officer during the early battles of the great war in Europe.

TROOP HORSE & TRENCH *by R.A. Lloyd*—The experiences of a British Lifeguardsman of the household cavalry fighting on the western front during the First World War 1914-18.

THE EAST AFRICAN MOUNTED RIFLES *by C.J. Wilson*—Experiences of the campaign in the East African bush during the First World War.

THE LONG PATROL *by George Berrie*—A Novel of Light Horsemen from Gallipoli to the Palestine campaign of the First World War.

THE FIGHTING CAMELIERS *by Frank Reid*—The exploits of the Imperial Camel Corps in the desert and Palestine campaigns of the First World War.

STEEL CHARIOTS IN THE DESERT *by S. C. Rolls*—The first world war experiences of a Rolls Royce armoured car driver with the Duke of Westminster in Libya and in Arabia with T.E. Lawrence.

WITH THE IMPERIAL CAMEL CORPS IN THE GREAT WAR *by Geoffrey Inchbald*—The story of a serving officer with the British 2nd battalion against the Senussi and during the Palestine campaign.

www.ingramcontent.com/pod-product-compliance
Lightning Source LLC
Chambersburg PA
CBHW021110090426

42738CB00006B/587